Following the Shepherd

Following the Shepherd

Janet Treat

WESTBOW
PRESS
P R E S S
A DIVISION OF THOMAS NELSON

ISBN: 978-1-4497-2201-2 (sc)
ISBN: 978-1-4497-2200-5 (e)

Library of Congress Control Number: 2011912200

WestBow Press books may be ordered through booksellers or by contacting:

WestBow Press
A Division of Thomas Nelson
1663 Liberty Drive
Bloomington, IN 47403
www.westbowpress.com
1-(866) 928-1240

All Scripture quotations, unless otherwise indicated, are taken from the New King James Version.

Printed in the United States of America

WestBow Press rev. date: 8/23/2011

Give thanks to the Lord, call on His name; make known among the nations what He has done. I Chronicles 16:8

It is all about You, Jesus, all about You.
I will worship You 'til my life is through.

Glory to Your Holy name.
You are always good and forever the same.

Unchanging, Light Giver, Promise Keeper-my all in all.
Your Word brings me hope and I rejoice in my call.

A call to take light and love to the people.
Until all the joy bells ring out in every steeple

"Holy is the Lamb. Glory to the Lamb.
Jesus, my Redeemer, who is the Great I Am."

I Can't Say No to Jesus

I can't say no to Jesus.
Not when He's my Master and Lord
His Spirit within gives direction.
He's my Shepherd, my King, my Adored.

To hurt Him with my disobedience,
Might cause the angels to cry.
I won't say No to Jesus.
For it's on Him I humbly rely.

Agreeing with Your word, dear Jesus
That by Your stripes I am healed.
I proclaim Your truth to the nations.
I know that in heaven it's sealed.

Jesus, You give me such peace.
And the world can't take it away.
You obeyed the Father completely,
That I might know Him today.

My heart sings songs of pure worship.
The joy of heaven is mine.
I want all to know Him and love Him.
No treasures on earth are so fine.

You spoke and gave me a promise.
I'd have strength for all of my days.
Stay close beside me, I'll follow
And go forth in sweet joyful praise.

Introduction and Acknowledgements

I wrote this book to preserve the true stories of my life, that others might gain insight and become confident followers of our beloved Shepherd, Jesus Christ.

I begin the book with my portrayal of the small, but powerful nation of Georgia. Along with this description and at the end of the book, I have added my depiction of the Mark IV Harvest ministry as it is today while we continue to minister to the precious children of Georgia.

We have come a long way. From having six attendance centers throughout the city of Tbilisi, we now have one beautiful school building for all twelve grades. To God be the glory. Great things He has done! With grateful hearts we give Him all the praise.

Thank you for giving to the Lord.
A heart-felt thank you goes to Sara Bennett, Dusty Treat, Reeta Treat, Mary Grace Coming and Sherri Ward. Without your encouragement and hard work, this book would not have become a reality. You gave of your expertise and time so willingly and selflessly. Keti Kurdiani (former graduate of SOT) is the brilliant front cover artist. Another big thanks goes to my wonderful husband, Earl, who patiently believed in me and challenged me to finish the task. I am so blessed to be his wife.

Most of all, I want to praise and thank the Lord Jesus Christ who gives such amazing grace and strength. He is my life and it is my desire that this book might bring Him pleasure as well as all who read it. I may be wrong, but sometimes, while I am writing, it almost seems He is smiling.

I am very grateful to the WestBow Press for their patience and encouragement that they gave me. To all my many awesome friends that prayed for me and encouraged me, as well as my wonderful family, I say thank you from the bottom of my heart.

vii

After years of learning to listen to the still, small voice of God and writing down what He shared with me through the Holy Spirit, I decided to write, in book form, some of the lessons I've learned from my fellowship with the Lord. All of the stories and poems are written down to help others experience the joy of close relationship with Him. It is my prayer that you will find a deep knowing of His great love for you from reading this book.

This book is a treasure chest of jewels written down to bring Him glory and for the purpose of giving hope and shining light into the dark places of the readers' hearts. The poems and stories I am sharing with you whisper treasures of truth which I have learned by closely following the Shepherd as He took me into His green pastures and beside the still waters of His presence.

CONTENTS

GEORGIA *on My Mind* — *1*

Chapter 1-Promises — **5**

TO MY FIVE SONS — *8*

Chapter 2-Answering the Call — **11**

LISTEN — *15*

The Biggest Loser Wins — *16*

HE WHO OVERCOMES — *18*

The First Healing Miracle — *20*

The Second Healing Miracle — *22*

WAITING — *24*

Chapter 3-The Shepherd Leads His Children — **25**

LIVING FOR JESUS — *28*

Chapter 4-The Knowing — **31**

Chapter 5-Never Alone — **33**

A TREASURED FRIEND — *36*

Chapter 6-Pressing Toward the Goal — **39**

HELP ME TO SEE — *44*

Chapter 7- Loss Turns to Gain — **47**

His Joy! — *51*

Chapter 8-All Things New — **53**

The Showing Story — *55*

THE GREAT EXCHANGE — *58*

Chapter 9- Obey and Be Blessed — **61**

The Long's Peak Climb Story — *64*

LIFE THROUGH OBEDIENCE — *66*

LOVE WHISPERS — *67*

Chapter 10-Worry Is a Sin — **69**

CONTENTMENT — *73*

MY SONG — *74*

UNDER HIS WINGS — *75*

Chapter 11-Right Thoughts – Right Behavior   **77**

    WORDS   *80*

    MARTHA AND MARY   *85*

Chapter 12-Abounding Love   **87**

Chapter 13-Journeys with Jan   **93**

    MY LIFE   *100*

Chapter 14-Builders   **103**

    The School of Tomorrow and Mark IV Harvest   *110*

GEORGIA ON My Mind

SAKARTVELO - LIVE FOREVER

What is Georgia? The name suggests southern charm, graceful and magnificent mansions, rolling green hills. This is not the Georgia of which I speak! Georgia is the tiny gem of a nation that is nestled down between the Black and the Caspian Seas. The hostile and formidable Russia to the north and Turkey to the south! Georgia is in a unique strategic, spiritual and geographical location. She is a place of such surpassing and exquisite beauty; from the sixteen thousand-foot striking Caucus mountain peaks to her valleys carpeted with the lovely wild flowers and laced with her rushing, clear mountain streams! Grandeur and rugged terrain are the features I most admire in her landscape for her beauty brings one reverently into pure worship of her Creator!

What is Georgia? She is a struggling democracy that is crying out to be allowed to become, to shine, to have peace amongst the nations of the world! One can not help but be proud of such a beautiful and astonishing people!

Georgia is mine! "How can you say that?" you cry. It is mine by appreciation, by love, and by appropriation, and by the seizure of her beauty and strength through living here so many days, nights and seasons for the past over nineteen years. It is mine by the fact that my family and I have suffered with these generous, intelligent, and warm people through many sorrows! We cried with them through the ending of the cruel civil war in the spring of 1992! We were on the first commercial airplane that was allowed to come into the aftermath of a bloody overthrow of the first president, Gamsakhurdia, and again during the merciless and brutal invasion by Russia into the incredibly beautiful Abkhazia in 1993, when over fifty-thousand of their people were murdered or displaced! Yes! She is mine, because our sons gave ammunition to some of the soldiers who were going to fight in that war! (Our youngest son was given the ammunition by a Georgian soldier friend.) Georgia is mine, because we endured the cold winters when Russia shut off the gas into Georgia and when the electricity was off more than on and we were happy with them when "something was running well."

Georgia is mine because we share in her sufferings and rejoice in her victories! Four of our five sons have lived in Georgia and the two youngest practically grew up there. They are grateful for the life-long Georgian friends they made there; some were with them when they were robbed and threatened! Through the dark years of muggings and crowded buses and through the terrifying days before "The Rose Revolution" when we prayed many prayers with our beloved Georgian brothers and sisters, we have endured alongside them! Together, we have wept and rejoiced in answered prayer!

Georgia is the dancer who is incredible in her strength, beauty and fierceness and always makes me want to cry in her intensely magnificent performances! Georgia is the piercingly independent and tough mountain people of Svaneti, the exceedingly hospitable and warm people of the country. She is in her succulent, spicy dishes that her ancestors created thousands of years ago, in her balconies that speak of her friendliness and fondness of sharing, in her gardens and in the abundant fruit of her land. Georgia is in her world-famous, delicious wines, made from the grapes of her prolific vineyards!

Throughout the centuries, Georgians have proven themselves to be strong and incredibly courageous! They have been invaded by nations many times over larger and seemingly more powerful than they. Yet, they endure! How can this be? They show their strength by their persistence, their determination and their warrior spirit, but more importantly they show their strength by their faith in God! He lifts up those that call upon Him in humility and faith! And this is why I can call Georgia mine, for I worship with Georgians in their ancient, magnificent churches and as we pray together and thank God together - we are one!

What is Georgia? She is the beautiful Georgian language that is one of the first thirteen written languages of the world. She is Rustaveli's "Knight in the Panther's Skin" and in the great works of her poets like Chavchavadze who showed such a deep faith in God, and tells about Georgia's faith in so many of his poems and writings!

Georgia is the splendid and glorious Orthodox Cathedrals and her faith through the centuries! Since Saint Nino brought Christianity to Georgia in 337 AD, she has been known as a Christian nation! Saint Nino, a young slave girl from Cappadocia, prayed for Queen Nana to be healed. God healed her and because of this miracle, King Miriam made a declaration of faith in God through Jesus Christ. He proclaimed Georgia Christian at that time!

Again, we might ask, "What is Georgia?" Georgia is music! May she never lose her song! She is in her superb, melodic singing that is so rich with ten-part harmonies, and beauty so splendid that it pierces the soul! Georgia is truly a unique and brilliant jewel of a nation that is only one-third the size of Colorado, but with a heart as big as the ocean! She is so delightful to the senses that one feels somehow "at home" there and yet visitors know in their hearts that only "true Georgians" can, in all honesty, call her theirs. May she endure and be blessed until the end of time!

Gaumarjos! Victory for Georgia! GOD BLESS GEORGIA!

PROMISES
CHAPTER 1

"The LORD is my shepherd."

It had been a warm and golden summer day in northwest Kansas, when the Lord first gave me a wonderful promise for our sons. A friend and I had taken our children to a park to play. As I was sitting under a tree reading my Bible and praying for our sons, I ran across a verse in Isaiah that seemed to leap off the page at me! It was Isaiah 54:13-*"All your sons will be taught by the LORD and great will be your children's peace."*

This glorious promise in Isaiah seemed to come alive in my heart and it has never lost its power. It is like a pledge to me and is not only for our children and their children, but also for the children in our Christian school in Georgia.

At that time, we had three sons and both Earl and I had committed our lives to bring them up for our Lord. They were healthy, strong, and active! Each day, I genuinely loved being a housewife and mother. Even though I had found much joy in teaching, I honestly didn't think I would go back to my teaching career, at least not until our children were raised. I discovered that being a wife and mother was even more fulfilling than any profession, even my beloved teaching.

It was just weeks later in the fall of the year that I found myself afraid and anxious. The late afternoon sun shone brightly across the wheat stubble fields, but my heart was heavy and there were tears in my eyes. Our third son, Daniel, was only a few months old. We were returning home from a meeting in a town near our farm. I remember looking down at his beautiful face as he was sleeping peacefully in his baby-sized car seat next to me. The afternoon sun glistened off his bright red hair and his long eyelashes lay upon his round pink cheeks. He seemed to be glowing!

The speaker at the meeting I had attended had talked about the appalling satanic worship services that were taking place in our area! It sounded so horrific and I felt sick to my stomach as she told of animal-blood rituals. Frightened and alarmed, I felt undone as I meditated upon her words. How could Earl and I raise our three wonderful sons to be secure and happy in such an evil world?

After arriving home from the meeting, I felt led to play one of our new record albums. It was one that I had not yet listened to closely. Still upset while nursing our baby boy, I began to listen to the anointed words of the song that was playing. The words went straight into my worried heart! The song was "Because He Lives" and the first verse penetrated my anxious thoughts and gave me back my peace and hope for the future.

"How sweet it is to hold our newborn baby and feel the pride and joy He gives. But greater still, the calm assurance, that this child can face uncertain days, because He lives!" Once more, our faithful God had heard the cry of this mother's heart and He answered me as He poured His balm and serenity over me. I knew we could trust Him each step of the way as we raised our sons for Him.

I believe had we not learned these lessons of trust and obedience to God's Word and had we not learned that we could trust Him completely, He would not have called us to go forth into other nations to take the Light of the Gospel through the open door of education. We learned so many years ago how to hear His voice and obey Him quickly. Someone has said, "The safest place to be is in the center of His will."

Our Five Sons

To My Five Sons

❖ I sit here in Moscow in our living room.
There's joy in my heart and no feeling of doom.
As I dream of our soon trip home to the States.
There's no doubt that God will care for our suitcases and crates.

❖ I'm so proud of you guys; there can be no doubt.
You each love the Lord and for this I do shout!
And smile when they say, "Five sons! Oh, dear me!"
For raising you up has been fun for I know the key.

❖ The key has been prayer and trusting each day.
I give you to Him as on my bed I do lay.
For I know that His promises for you are so true.
His peace is for each of you, our beautiful Treat crew.

❖ There is no place on earth He will take you each to,
Be it back here in Moscow, Tbilisi, or Peru.
Where He won't protect and give you joy and His love.
Your steps will be sure, says our Father above.

❖ The world needs such men as the five of you sons.
I'm your mom, I can tell you and I don't need a pun.
You each are so special and I love you so much.
Keep right on serving and giving; you each know His touch.

❖ Now, soon Doug will give me a daughter, it's true.
She's lovely and pure like a flower to you.
And I thank God He's chosen her to be yours.
There are four more just right for you other sweet boys.

❖ So, don't be in a hurry; just wait on His plan.
He has a woman who's perfect for 'most every man.
You may meet her in Kansas or in Amsterdam.
Don't worry or fret, just look to the Lamb.

❖ Well, as I sit here and dream of our reunion so soon.
I just can't help smiling and singing a tune.

It's our song and we'll sing it together at home.
Please, "Shine Jesus Shine" there and wherever we roam.

❖ Now, I cannot leave out your really great dad.
He's just as proud as I am of the five of you lads.
I pray you'll be like him in faith and integrity, too.
God will say, "Well done!" to you all, if to Him you'll be true.
With much love~ Mother   (July 1992)

ANSWERING THE CALL
Chapter 2

"I shall not want."

Although neither of the boys had complained about leaving their friends and all they held dear, Dusty had begged us to let him take his beloved cat, Buffy, to Georgia. We knew we couldn't bring the cat, but one of my students at the Christian school where I taught said she felt that God had told her she was to keep the cat for Dusty. Although it was painful to leave Buffy, once Dusty knew in his heart that God had called us all to go, he didn't complain. After we returned home for the summer of 1993, Dusty got Buffy back. She lived twelve more years until she was nineteen. We have discovered that when we are asked to give up anything to obey our Lord, He will, in some way, return it or give us something better.

I knew in my heart that the missionary call to start a Christian school in the city of Tbilisi, Georgia, would not be without suffering and loss! Philippians chapter 3 verse 10 says "that I may know Him and the power of His resurrection, and the fellowship of His sufferings, being conformed to His death." This verse had seemed etched upon my heart as we said, "Yes!" to the call He had spoken to us so clearly, just one and a half years before. It wasn't like He hadn't prepared us for the call, but still, it certainly had been so completely unexpected!

The first "call" came to me while writing in my journal, one evening in April 1988. The words startled me and my heart skipped a beat! What He said was to me just incredible! "I am calling you to a higher call; to do something that you have never even dreamed about. Your whole family is involved in this."

I loved my job as teacher of the Kindergarten/First Grade classes in our church's Christian school. Earl had turned down a job as principal in the school a few years before because we had purchased a food business where he produced popped wheat.

After God had spoken to me through what I wrote in my journal, I looked out the window of our comfortable bedroom into the backyard of our charming home just outside of Loveland, Colorado. I could see the gorgeous tall trees that graced our three acres. We were still landscaping our property with flower gardens, a gazebo on the edge of the river, and a winding stone path that went through a climbing rose-covered arbor. I felt some fear and regret that God must be calling us to leave all that behind, for we had humbly asked Him to be anchor and Captain of our lives. To disobey Him was just incomprehensible to us both.

When Earl returned with the boys from a meeting at our church, I asked if I could read him something before turning off the light. As I read the words from my journal he looked at me with complete disbelief! He could not even speak! We committed all this to the Lord, knowing that if it was Him, He would begin to show us the way He wanted us to go. He was Jehovah Shalom, our peace and our faithful Shepherd and Friend.

The second call came during a teacher's conference for ACE schools in Denver a year after the first "call". I was sitting next to our pastor as we listened to the founder of ACE curriculum who was the speaker. He showed us slides of parents and children in Russia who were asking for people to come and set up Christian schools in their newly freed nation of Russia. I saw on their faces such deep hope that this might be for their children and my heart felt like it was breaking. I was weeping and deeply moved by the power of the Holy Spirit.

Our pastor leaned over and asked me what was happening. I answered with conviction, "Someday, Earl and I will go to other parts of the world and start Christian schools." These words came from my spirit and not from my mind. We were both utterly amazed!

We had another delightful year, pursuing our careers and raising our five wonderful boys! We entertained often and our five sons loved living on the banks of a mountain river where they had tubing parties throughout the summer months.

∞

It was now 1991. David, our oldest son, had left home five years earlier at the age of eighteen to follow God's direction in his life to become a missionary. He was totally sold out to Him. He managed to come home that summer for a brief vacation. Doug, twenty-one, was home after graduating from the Bible college, Christ for the Nations. He had been privileged to be part of their drama team which went to the Mardi Gras in New Orleans that spring where he saw hundreds come to a saving knowledge of our Lord. Daniel, seventeen, was preparing to finish his senior year in our wonderful Christian school in Fort Collins and he planned to attend the Youth with a Mission Bible training school in Neah Bay, Washington in the fall. Dathan was fifteen and enjoying High School in the same Christian School and Dusty, eleven, was in the fifth grade.

It was on a hike up in the Rocky Mountain National Park when we talked to our sons about the call to go to a former Communist country to start a Christian school and each one agreed to join us in praying about it. They did not seem surprised or dismayed, but were very serious and knew that we respected each of them and that we felt it was important that they each knew that this was of God. In just a matter of a week or so, each of the boys told us that they felt that this was a call for the family and were willing to go as God led us!

Later, in June of that year, our pastor attended a conference for Christian schools. At his return, he excitedly announced to our church in Fort Collins that he was convinced that our church was called to send a couple to Russia to start a Christian school. He said that a man had spoken at the meeting asking America not to forget them! "Send us schools for our children!" As I heard these words, a feeling much like electricity went through me, as my mind grasped the reality of God's assignment for us.

That very evening, we answered the call, not only to our God, but to our church, as well! Yes! We would go, but only God could help us prepare to leave by January, for we all knew that the time to go was NOW! There was much to do! Someone must be hired to manage Hilary Mills Popped Wheat, the business Earl owned, and a teacher must be found to take my place in the school. We ourselves must prepare to teach English to non-English speaking children. So much to learn and so little time!

LISTEN

Quiet your heart
...and listen.

Wait and then start
...to listen.

Find a peaceful place
...and listen.

No noise in this space
...just listen.

He waits there for you
...to listen.

Every word He speaks is true
...won't you listen.

Love whispers soft
...shush, now listen.

It comes without cost
...only listen.

He says to forgive all
...when you listen.

Anger creates stress- hear Him call
... draw near and - **Listen.**

The Biggest Loser Wins

One night, as I watched "The Biggest Loser" show on television I was inspired! As I watched people grow in their perception of themselves and each other, I saw them begin to truly love themselves and conversely begin to know how to love each other. I was moved to tears as I watched their tenacity and endurance grow through the pain of losing fat and gaining muscle.

I think this show is so well-liked because it's a real show with real people who are motivated to become better and stimulated to climb higher than they ever thought possible. They give the viewers hope that they can change as well.

I was stirred in my heart when I watched them grow in their relationships with one another. Especially inspiring to me was the way the teams pulled together, encouraging one another, without partiality. "All for one and one for all!" One of the contests tonight happened to be a semi-truck pull. Watching how the teams began to work together, using every ounce of strength as they pulled huge trucks down the road. An incredible scene!

The world is crying out for something more than "churchianity." People yearn for the powerful presence of God that is measurable and viable in their lives. They desire to see people who are over comers, who persevere when the pressure is on. People who overcome the desire to give in and quit. He promises much to those who will overcome in the days to come.

" He who is holy. He who is true, He who has the key of David. He who opens and no one shuts and shuts and no one opens" I know your works. See, I have set before you an open door and no one can shut it for you have a little strength, have kept My word and have not denied My name. Because you have kept My command to persevere, I also will keep you from the hour of trial which shall come upon the whole world to test those who dwell on the earth. Behold, I am

coming quickly! Hold fast what you have, that no one may take your crown. He who overcomes, I will make him a pillar in the temple of My God. To Him who overcomes I will grant to sit with Me on the throne as I also overcame and sat down with My Father on His throne." (Rev. 3:7,8,10, 12a NKJV)

HE WHO OVERCOMES

May I be an over comer,
In the days to come
Faithful to the end,
As in this race I run.

Don't worry over those whose run is faster.
Your strength indeed is small,
I will be all you need,
I'll come quickly when you call.

I'm your Shepherd and I'll lead you.
Be alert, stay by My side.
Stay ever beneath My wing.
In Me you shall humbly abide.

Nothing can take My love from you.
Through faith you've been given grace.
Seek always to serve and bless Me.
And keep your eyes upon My face.

Before long a day is coming,
When all sorrows here will cease.
It shall never again grow dark
And the light will surely increase.

So look up and stay alert, My child.
You must stay tough in the fight.
Don't give up, keep moving ahead
Fight on with all your might

Soon He is coming in all His glory
We'll join the angels with our praise.
And thank Him throughout the ages.
Our voices we will raise.

The door is open to His glory.
Soon we'll cast our crowns at His feet.
He is worthy to receive glory, honor, and power.
Our worship of Him will never cease.

Saying "Holy Holy Holy"
Lord God Almighty -Who was and is to come. (Revelation 4:8a,)

The First Healing Miracle

In the fall of 1975, I was baking in our wonderful old farm kitchen in NW Kansas. Our fourth beautiful son, Dathan Jessie, nicknamed DJ, was around a month old and Daniel was two. I had strapped DJ into his carrier and set him up on the kitchen counter. Daniel was "helping" me make cookies. As I walked over to get something from the refrigerator, I suddenly heard a crash and a piercing scream almost simultaneously.

What I saw when I turned around took my breath away! Daniel had stood up on the cabinet and reached up to the top shelf for an empty jelly jar. It had slipped from his little fingers and crashed to the floor, shattering into sharp, lethal pieces. He had fallen, head-first onto a jagged piece of glass, piercing his head just above the hair line. It looked as if the glass had pierced his sweet head at least a half-inch. I gingerly pulled it from his scalp and ran with him into the bathroom where his blood quickly saturated a big bath towel. His screams, now along with DJ's frightened cries, could have been heard as far away as our barn, I think. It was terrifying!

I took another towel and wrapped it around his head and ran to call Earl who was teaching in a school which was nearly thirty miles away. I knew I couldn't take both babies to the hospital alone so I was about to call 911 when God spoke to my heart quite clearly.

He said, "I will heal him if you ask!" I put the phone down and ran to pick-up our screaming son, Daniel. I laid my hand on the now blood-saturated towel on his little head and asked that God touch and heal him. Immediately he stopped crying! I washed the blood from his head and the gash was closed as if someone had pulled it together and stitched it up, perfectly. There was no soreness, no more bleeding, and Daniel was completely at peace, as was his baby brother. I could even comb his hair over it and he didn't feel any pain! All of the pain was completely gone! To this day, he has the scar where his hair does not grow to remind him of God's awesome power to heal. It was the first of many miracles in our lives.

ℒ

The Treat Family

The Second Healing Miracle

His precious blood cleanses from all our sin
And we become new because of Him.
Living under the shadow of the Cross of our Lord
Knowing true peace comes from The Adored.

There is no more shame and no more stain.
We can hold up our heads and sing out the refrain
"In the cross. In the cross. Be my glory ever."
Singing His songs for He is my Deliverer.

We rejoice in His loving, healing touch.
He's always the same and He loves us so much.
It was in my first class of girls and boys.
There was a special fellow who made a lot of noise.

I sat him near me- up close to the front,
So he could learn better instead of doing his stunts.
One day, he didn't come to the school.
He had fallen off a roof…now this wasn't cool.

He'd ruptured his spleen: they had to operate.
He lived through the night, but was in a very bad state
His spleen was destroyed; it had to be taken.
He could live without it, but would be weak and shaken.

We went to the hospital and prayed for God's healing touch.
We talked to him about how God loved him ever so much
In a week, his doctors x-rayed him before he could go.
And found out God had made him **perfectly whole.**

He had a new spleen that was working just fine.
We all knew God's healing touch came just in time!
Today, He is married, has a child with another on the way.
He is a strong man and thankful for His life every day.

Waiting

They that wait upon the Lord
Sing a song with one accord~
Hosanna to the King of Kings.
No matter what tomorrow brings
…I will trust Him and not be afraid!

They that wait upon the Lord
Extol the Lord their adored!
He is the Almighty God to save
And His Word He freely gave.
…I will trust Him and not be afraid!

They that wait upon the Lord
Proclaim His truth to the World.
There is no life without Him.
He heals, delivers, and forgives all sin.
…I will trust Him and not be afraid!

"God's loyal love couldn't have run out
His merciful love couldn't have dried up.
They're created new every morning.
How great your faithfulness! Lamentations 3:22-24 Message

As we quietly wait, abiding in the Vine, our Lord brings us into more fruitfulness and more of His glory than we ever dreamed possible! We can be absolutely certain that He has the perfect plan for each of our lives. … we can trust Him!

THE SHEPHERD LEADS HIS CHILDREN
Chapter 3

"He makes me to lie down in green pastures."

"Not that I speak in regard to need, for I have learned in whatever state I am, to be content." (Phil. 4:11)

"How would you like to go the Georgia to build a school?" Earl asked me. I thought he meant the state of Georgia, USA. I was quite puzzled. The call from God had been to go to the former Soviet Union. I was surprised as I thought he was talking about teaching in the state of Georgia.

Earl, along with our pastor and two other leaders from our church traveled to Moscow for several days in October, 1991. We were all trying to decide where we were to plant a Christian school in the former Soviet Union. Most of us felt that we would be sent to start the school in the Ukraine. However, on the way to Kiev with Dr. Howard, the founder of our Christian school curriculum, they went through Tbilisi, Georgia. Before that trip, we had not even heard of the country of Georgia.

It was in the capital city of Tbilisi, one night in early October that God spoke clearly to Earl about where He would have us minister! Earl could not sleep. Jetlag and an almost visible tension in this city of a million and half people made it impossible to relax enough to sleep. He heard low angry voices in the room next to him and felt that the men were planning something illegal as their voices were so sinister sounding. (Later, he realized that they were indeed planning a revolution to oust President Gomsahodia.)

He was reading the Bible and looking out over the sleeping city. The passage he was reading was from Psalm 78: 1-8. He "saw" the faces of Georgian children and he cried as he realized that he was truly "falling in love" with the people of Georgia! The next day, the Vice-Minister of Education in Georgia signed the contract that Dr. Howard had brought to start the Christian school in January. That Georgian leader turned to Earl and said, "I want *you* to be the one to come and start our school!"

This was just the first of many confirmations that we were, indeed, to go to Georgia!

"What was he saying?" My doctor was telling me that although the fibroid tumor that I carried in my womb was not cancerous, it must be removed if we were going to live out of the United States for a long period of time. He told me that it might rupture and cause a lot of problems and could even be life-threatening if left! He told me that I must have the operation no later than October, if I was to be strong enough to leave the States by the last of December.

After much prayer and consideration, Earl and I agreed to the surgery, but the night before the scheduled operation, I was not so sure that I wanted to go through with it! Confusion and fear plagued my mind, for I knew that this would be a painful and traumatic surgery that would surely affect my strength for some time.

It was nearly midnight and while we were praying and trying to determine if we should go through with the procedure, our wonderful friends from Kansas came to the door. I went to answer and show them to their room. They had lovingly driven out to care for me during and after the surgery. When I came back into the bedroom, I could feel the sweet sense of God's presence!

"What has happened?" I asked Earl breathlessly.

"Right after you left the room, I felt the bed move and knew that Someone was sitting on it," he answered! There was a tangible, sweet presence of the Lord which imparted a quiet peace into our hearts. We fell asleep with the assurance that God was leading us to go ahead with the surgery.

Later, I was so thankful for the confidence God had given us to have the surgery. There were several complications and a very painful recovery period that left me weak and drained. However, my healing came speedily and by Christmas Day, 1991; Earl, Doug, Dathan, Dusty, and I were on our way to Moscow, answering the Shepherds call.

LIVING FOR JESUS

If I could tell you something that would change your life today!
And give you peace of mind no matter what you hear folks say!
Would you listen and take heart, my friend, for I would bless you, too?
And send a hug with wishes sweet to you and you and you!

God gave us minds that we can use
To choose the best each day.
And we don't have to let a soul
Take this precious gift away.

Your mind is that which helps you think
To analyze and choose....
His guidance and His wisdom, too,
Is there for you to use.

Whenever there's an obstacle
That you need to rise above,
It helps to overcome it with
An attitude of love.

Anger never solves a thing
And stress will bring us down,
But love unlocks the doorway
Where all hope and faith are found.

Please don't hide your light in the shadows,
Nor allow it to grow faint or dim.
Let it shine with all its glory-
And proclaim your love for Him.

So, whenever life seems unfair
And things don't go your way,
Don't choose to shout and carry on,
Instead begin to pray.

After you tell Him what's on your heart
He'll give you hope and rest.
We realize, though life seems hard,
That our Father knows what's best.

THE KNOWING
CHAPTER 4

"He leads me beside still waters."

"And my God shall supply all your need according to His riches in glory by Christ Jesus. (Philippians 4:19)

Someone leaned over Earl's shoulder at church and handed him a note that told of the civil war that had just broken out in Tbilisi, Georgia! The newly formed republic had elected President Gomsahodia and he had not been able to lead this struggling little country that was still under the thumb of the Russian Bear, and extremely corrupt! Two mafia groups had attacked the small Georgian army. Later, President Gomsahodia was mysteriously killed.

After the first shock and disbelief, we both had a calm assurance that we were to go as planned, for our Lord had definitely called! We were to leave on Christmas Day which was two days away. All the preparations were made. We were packed! Earl had hired a man to run his popped wheat company and the Christian school where I had taught for seven and a half years had my replacement. God would go before us; we would follow!

Many signs had been given us indicating we were to go forth into the harvest field of The Republic of Georgia, former Soviet Georgia! One of those was **"The Sandals"**-

Ellen was teaching the Kindergarten/First Grade classes with me that fall semester of 1991. She told me one morning that God had spoken to her and she was to buy me a pair of shoes to wear in Georgia! What a blessing it had been to make the trip to a nice shoe store in downtown Fort Collins where she felt she was to purchase my shoes.

There were two pairs of shoes that I was trying to choose from that afternoon. Ellen would not let me look at the price and she insisted that I was to have the very best pair in the store. After much deliberation and prayer, I picked the navy blue, well-built walking sandals. The salesman was so impressed that she was buying these shoes as a gift for me and that I would be starting a Christian school in a former Communist country, that he gave her a discount!

After we left the store, Ellen told me that she had purchased this same pair of shoes for herself and would be wearing them to teach in each day! We both felt that when we put our shoes on each morning we should pray for each other, our schools, and our students. I wore those blessed sandals hundreds of miles in Georgia during the next two years.

"How beautiful on the mountains are the feet of them that bring good news."

NEVER ALONE
CHAPTER 5

"He restores my soul."

It was Christmas Day 1991, and we all noisily hurried into Stapleton Airport in Denver along with all of our suitcases and crates. Many of our friends had given up their Christmas morning traditions to see us off to "Russia" or wherever we ended up! We were singing Christmas carols in the deserted corridors and some were blowing bubbles. Everyone was laughing, except Earl! He was so concerned that we would miss our flight or not get all our baggage checked in. Also, he thought we were too noisy, attracting too much attention.

Most of our friends had never traveled outside of the USA, so they were quite nervous for us, and it was very hard to say "Goodbye!" that cool December day when our lives were forever changed! These were our closest friends and we felt sad to leave them, yet so sure that this was God's will for us. We knew He would care for them and us when we were on opposite sides of the globe! It seemed surreal! I remember the big hugs and tears through the smiles, and last "good-byes" that said so much more than just the words.

No one knew if we would have enough to eat in Russia as the economy was quite unstable. There were reports of empty shops and long bread lines everywhere. But, "Friends are friends forever if the Lord is the Lord of them" and so we turned our backs on them and all we had ever known, to walk through the gate and down the corridor to our plane.

A kind and perceptive flight attendant had worn Santa socks that Christmas morning and he kept coming by letting Dusty and Dathan pull the string so that "Jingle Bells" would play. We laughed and the boys thought them so clever. Along with other things, this nice young man helped them get over their nervousness in flying for the first time. None of us slept much on the long flight over the Atlantic to Paris. However, while we waited for our next flight on to Moscow, we all napped in the hard airport chairs, sleeping several hours. Although, we were exhausted and miserable in our bodies, we knew that our Shepherd was leading us and that He would continue to meet our every need!

Psalm 100~"*Make a joyful noise all the lands. Serve the Lord with gladness. Come before His presence with singing. Know ye that the LORD, He is God. It is He that has made us and not we ourselves. We are the sheep of His pasture. Enter into His gates with thanksgiving and into His courts with praise. Be thankful unto Him and bless His name. For the Lord is good. His truth endures to all generations.*"

As I dozed on the uncomfortable Paris airport chairs, my mind traveled back to earlier Kansas days. I remembered the day I was setting the table in our big, beautiful farm kitchen after preparing dinner for the six of us. I had been to a women's Bible study, cleaned our lovely old farm house, washed two loads of clothes, and made an apple pie for supper, and helped David and Doug with their homework. Earl came in from the barn where he hand-milked our two milk cows, and sat down at the table to say grace. After he took a bite of the mashed potatoes he asked, "What would you say if I told you I think we are to start a Christian school here in this area?" I was surprised as he was so well-liked at the public school and he enjoyed teaching there.

He had noticed that our son, David, who was in the second grade, was being influenced by the other children in his class in ways that we did not want him to go. He had even gotten into trouble with some of the boys who were caught smoking on the school playground. Although he was not smoking, he had brought the matches for the other boys. Our highest aim in life was to train up our sons to be honest and well-adjusted; living for the Lord.

Just days before, Earl had been asked to take the job of school principal in the school where he taught, with a nice raise in salary and all the benefits that went with it! Even though it was hard to give up the financial security of that job, we were convinced that he must turn it down and we began to prepare to start the first Christian school in our farming community.

Was God preparing us for something bigger?

A TREASURED FRIEND

…is what I have in you.

A treasured friend you will always be.
A friend that is rare and helps me to see,
How much God loves both you and me.
And teaches me what it is to be free.
…is what I have in you.

You know me well and yet you stay,
Close beside me in the heat of the day.
Through the good times and even the bad,
Your hand in mine makes me feel glad.
…is what I have in you.

I will sing of your love in the darkest night.
When troubles come or in the morning light.
Your laughter takes me to a place that is higher.
And gives me such joy and a life-giving fire.
…is what I have in you.

Your friendship is more beautiful than the rarest jewel.
You refresh my spirit like a life-giving pool.
With your hand in mine, I can face my tomorrow,
I can go through every joy and the deepest sorrow.
…is what I have in you.

I am lifted up with the sound of your name.
For you give me hope, never ridicule nor blame.

I'll always thank God for you, dearest friend of mine.
You're the best and I know it, for you help me to shine.
...is what I have in you

PRESSING TOWARD THE GOAL
Chapter 6

*"He leads me in the paths of righteousness
for His name sake."*

*"Not that I have already attained, or am already perfected; but I press on,
that I may lay hold of that for which Christ Jesus has also laid hold of me."*
(Philippians 3:12)

The tarmac was extremely rough as our ancient Aeroflot plane landed in Tbilisi, Georgia, on that cold and windy early morning flight. Most of the Georgian passengers clapped loudly for the safe landing and our twelve year old son, Dusty, whose head was on my lap, jumped awake from his restless sleep. I felt him shiver as he looked out the dirty window upon the dark airport.

It was February 17, 1992, and the civil war that had torn the city into ruin was just over. The little country of Georgia was in turmoil, after this violent revolution and expulsion of the first elected President, Gamsakhurdia. All the passengers exited the plane nervously. I was not prepared for the gale of cold wind that seemed to tear at us as we walked out onto the steps. Holding tightly to the freezing rail, we stumbled down into the darkness wondering if we would survive living in this extremely dark and cold land!

Although anxious, we were grateful to God for bringing us to this unique and beautiful country. We were very certain that God had called us here and was orchestrating everything, including the many miracles we had experienced thus far! It was thrilling to be on this first passenger flight into Georgia since the war! George, our Georgian friend and co-worker, had single-handedly put together the flight at the enormous Sheremetyevo International Airport in Moscow, after our flight was canceled due to the crew refusing to fly into this dangerous and war-torn country. Also, there was the lack and expense of petrol.

After our scheduled flight to Georgia had been cancelled, George had somehow hired a crew and procured a plane. We had sat all day beside the small mountain of luggage that held our precious curriculum for the school. We were waiting and praying that we might find a way to get to Tbilisi, the capital of the tiny country of Georgia, knowing God had called us. We prayed for a miracle.

It was late afternoon when George announced on the intercom that anyone wanting to fly to Tbilisi must ,come to the special window where he was selling tickets. All the tickets quickly sold and the seats were all filled! After our first crew quit, he hired a new pilot. At last, fifteen hours after our scheduled flight, we were all seated on the plane. George announced on the plane's intercom that the pilot would not fly without more money and each person was to give more rubles. The amount the pilot demanded was around one US dollar. George used Earl's hat to collect the extra fee.

I remember praying for safety, as I watched the workers try to thaw ice off the wings so that our pilot could get the massive ancient plane off the ground! We all breathed a sigh of relief when we lifted off at 2 AM that cold winter morning in Russia! Little did we know that this was the first of many such traveling adventures in the former Soviet Union. Some would be even more exciting and dangerous!

The darkness of the city was not only caused by the lack of electricity; nor was the coldness in the air only the result of a late winter storm, but the lack of hope and peace had brought a despair that was tangible over the city of a million and a half people. We were convinced that our Lord had sent us to these people to bring His hope, love, and His Light back into their hearts. Nevertheless, the task seemed insurmountable in our present state of exhaustion!

We were taken to what seemed to me to be a small barn-like room where bullet holes had shattered some of the filthy windows and the howling wind pushed into the fairly small space provided for the international passengers.

40

Along with several other passengers, the four of us sat on old chairs and benches around a small kerosene stove that seemed to do nothing to penetrate the frigid air in the room!

Again, Earl and I prayed for safety as we heard gun shots in the distance. We knew that no one would be able to come to the airport to pick us up for several hours, as there was a night curfew in Tbilisi. It was only 4 AM and the curfew wouldn't lift until 6 AM. A small, cute puppy was lying close to what seemed to be the only heat in the airport and Dusty picked it up and held it close. As the cuddly puppy fell asleep on his lap, Dusty settled down against me and slept fitfully during the two hours we waited for the school director to come pick us up. Dr. M. was the Vice Minister of Education of Georgia. Earl had met him when he had traveled to Georgia in October of 1991.

We were concerned for our sixteen year old son, Dathan. Cold and exhausted, he was nodding as he also huddled on the bench close to the open fire. I shivered as anxious thoughts seemed to attack my mind. I tried to push the fear out and let God give me His peace while we waited.

Our lives had not always been easy. We were both raised on Kansas farms. I was born and raised in southeast Kansas and Earl in the opposite corner of the state. We met at college and as both of us had committed our lives to the Lord Jesus while quite young, we were praying for just the right mate. Even on our very first date, we both were pretty certain that God was granting our desire. Soon, we fell deeply in love and in a little over a year we were married, just seven days after our college graduations. After our gorgeous church wedding we began our lives together in an apartment near Earl's parents' home.

We obtained teaching jobs in the Kansas City area for the next school year. Our love for each other was deep and we were convinced that our marriage would be built on the Lord Jesus Christ and that He would guide us, always. He has proved Himself faithful throughout the forty-five plus years of our marriage. He has been the constant in our relationship. A Rock that we can depend upon and a secure dwelling place of safety.

The first summer of our married life, Earl helped his father with the farming. Many days I spent the long, lonely hours in our small dark apartment, longing for the trees and water that I was so accustomed to in southeast Kansas. Our love for each other was glorious, but I remember driving to the only river north of our small town and sitting under the big trees sobbing as I was so homesick. Little did I know that this was just a small preparation for the move we would make to the other side of the world, nearly 30 years later!

Soon, we moved to Kansas City into a beautiful, furnished apartment. Joyfully, we began our first married years in the teaching professions we loved so much! Our days were full and very demanding! Earl had a long drive through the city to his high school teaching job and although we lived only five miles from my school, I had to drive on a busy interstate each day, which was a bit scary for this farm girl!

I loved my classes, although they were huge and the challenge was great! I had from thirty-eight to forty students in the morning and the same in the afternoon. The school was set-up in a team teaching arrangement, so there was only a bookcase separating the other kindergarten classroom with the same number of students. The team teacher that taught with me hated teaching and refused to help plan or work with me. She repeated my lessons and I had nearly all of our 80 students for the reading and music classes, as well as all recesses! I had no breaks and being young and inexperienced, there was always stress. However, God had given me such a desire to teach well and I loved the children, so the year was truly a great delight for me!

My co-worker soon quit and a new teacher hired. The girl that took her place was a wonderful teacher. Sharon and I enjoyed working together for the rest of that year and the next. Still, the job of keeping up with so many students and their parents was very difficult. I certainly didn't guess that I was gaining the information and expertise that would help me later in the former Soviet Union!

In the late summer of 1966, after spending time farming back in northwest Kansas, Earl joined the Army National Guard. The Viet Nam war was escalating and other young teachers were being called to duty. He was a very gentle young man and the thought of killing other young men was appalling to him. He hoped to escape an assignment to serve in the war, but he wanted to do his duty for his country.

We joyfully found that we were expecting a baby in September and we hoped he would be able to go in time to be back home for the birth of our baby. However, the Army didn't call Earl up until spring and his leaving was a hard separation for us both.

When summer break started, I traveled to Maryland to be with Earl for a month. We lived in an old hotel near the Aberdeen Proving Grounds in Maryland where he was stationed. Leaving him to go back home to have our first baby without him was so awfully difficult.

However, we continued to learn that God's plans are always good, even though they are not always free from pain and loss. Earl passed the tests with high enough scores to show the army that he had already learned the subjects in his college classes. He arrived home, after driving over one thousand miles straight through, just three days before the birth of our first beautiful baby boy, David, on August 24, 1967.

Open my eyes that I may see wonderful things in Your law.
(Psalm 119:18) So we fix our eyes not on what is seen, but on what is unseen.
For what is seen is temporary, but what is unseen is eternal. (2 Corinthians
4:18)

HELP ME TO SEE

I want to experience Your glory.
...Oh Lord. Help me to see.
Make me a pure vessel You flow through, freely.
...Lord, help me to see.
Closet me away into the secret places of humility.
...And, Lord, won't you help me to see?
Give me your grace, wisdom and tranquility.
...Lord, help me to see.
I repent and renounce my sin; make me free.
...Help me to see.
I draw near to You and You draw near to me.
...Oh, help me to see.
May Your love control my mind easily.
...And, Lord, help me to see.
Help me to keep the outflow of my life in motion, continually.
...Lord, help me to see.
May I always be kind and forgiving, even to my enemy.
...Help me to see.
I would eat at Your table, Lord, and at Your well, drink deeply.
...Just, please Lord, help me to see.
I'll seek peace and resist the devil; this is a key.
...With eyes opened that I might see.
In You, Lord, my soul shall rejoice, constantly.
...Oh, Lord, help me to see.
If I am to be a vessel of purity,
...Then, oh Lord, I must be able to see.
I will praise You Lord when it's hard and when it's very easy.
...Help me, just help me to see.

Oh, Lord, flow freely through me
...And help us all to have eyes that can see...Your face and into eternity.

LOSS TURNS TO GAIN
CHAPTER 7

"Yea, though I walk through the valley of the shadow of death, I will fear no evil for Thou art with me."

"But what things were gain to me, these I have counted loss for Christ. Yet indeed I also count all things loss for the excellence of the knowledge of Christ Jesus, my Lord, for whom I have suffered the loss of all things, and count them as rubbish, that I may gain Christ." (Philippians 3:7, 8)

When we left America on Christmas day, 1991, we knew that Lois, our precious friend and our pastor's wife, was extremely ill with cancer. Yet, when we had gone into the church office on Christmas Eve afternoon to say "Goodbye!" to her and our pastor, she had such a radiant smile on her face! It gave us hope for we had fervently prayed that God would heal her completely.

The next time I saw that smile, it was even more glowing. You see I didn't see her with my natural eyes! It was on an early Monday morning in March, 1991. I had awakened from a vivid dream. A beautiful dream and more real than any dream I had ever experienced. We were in Tbilisi, Georgia and the presence of the Lord in our bedroom was palpable. Earl also awakened and seeing tears on my cheeks, he questioned me.

"Lois is in heaven," I told him. "I saw her face and it was glowing with the most dazzling smile I have ever seen! She spoke to me and said, 'It's OK, Janie. It's OK. It's beautiful here!'"

Two days later, we received the email from our pastor telling us that she had passed away around 5 PM MT on Sunday evening, which would have been our 6 AM Monday morning, in Georgia. Days later, I asked the Lord why He had allowed Lois to come to me and He replied, "It was her request." It was a gift of tremendous value and I can't thank God enough!

Lois had been diagnosed with inoperable cancer, the same week that we were called to leave our home and all we knew and "go forth to build Christian schools for our Lord." We knew that He was calling both of us to a death-type experience. Hers' was physical, while mine was death to self; to all I'd ever known.

Our pastor called us to come to church early for the mid-week service, so that the elders and wives could anoint Lois with oil and pray for her healing. She came early into the church that night and I remember she sat down a few pews ahead of me. I asked the Lord what I should say to her. I recalled some cards I had recently put in my purse. The first one I pulled out said, "No matter what you may have to go through in this life, just remember you have a friend who is praying for you." As I gave her the card, we embraced and I spoke into her ear these words, "It is just to know Christ. Through the power of His resurrection and fellowship of His suffering… it is just to know Him!"

I shall never forget her words to me. "Yes, and Janie, I am so excited!"

(At that same time-From my journal…March 2, 1992)
"Put upon me your beautiful, spotless, glorious Robe of Righteousness and give unto me a meek and quiet spirit. I know that we will fail here if we do not let our old natures be crucified. We must allow You, Jesus, to dwell in us and do in us and through us what you want done in Tbilisi, Georgia. It seems we made a terrible mistake. But You don't lie and You don't make mistakes, so I will believe! I will die to self for only then will I begin to really live for You! I must! You will live out and through me, Oh, Blessed Jesus. I love You, Jesus! Heal our bodies and strengthen them and make us wise and understanding."

Later that same day: "My daughter, do you not feel the comfort of the old wool shawl around your shoulders?" (A precious lady that we had met in Moscow had placed the shawl around my neck one extremely cold day and given it as a gift of love.) "This is a symbol of my loving, warm, care over you. Relax and rest in it. Do not fret, grow fearful, or become anxious in any way. You are My vessel, fit for the Master's use. Many souls will come to know Me through you in this place."

The first loss to me came at the tender age of seven with the death of my beautiful mother. She had been diagnosed with leukemia when I was a baby and told she had a year at the most to live. But Mother was a fighter and she lived six more years. My wonderful father, my eleven year old brother, Billy, her parents and hundreds of friends, felt deep loss when she left us for glory that day in March, 1951.

Just like I had done everyday since Mother had gotten too weak to walk much, I ran into her room after arriving home from our one-room school house to tell her about my day in second grade. However, when I couldn't get her awake (She was in a coma.) I became quite alarmed!

Our godly, paternal grandmother was there and she gently took Billy and me to the kitchen where she told us Mother was not going to wake up here with us, but that she would awaken in Heaven and that she would be perfectly well. I was amazed! My sense of excitement and joy far surpassed any deep sadness at my own loss at that time. God's grace brought me through.

We had been praying for Mother's healing for so long. I was incredulous that she was really going to be healed! Grandma said that she would have no more pain and be so happy with Jesus! I was trembling with joy and anticipation; not for me, of course, but for my precious mother! At that time, there was no sense of loss, only deep peace and a comfort that only the Holy Spirit could give a little girl's heart at a time like this. I am extremely grateful for the grace that our Lord gave to us all.

We were all around her bed as the doctor told us that it would not be long. Her mother and father on one side, my brother and our dad standing at the end of the bed, I was there beside her and the doctor was sitting on the bed taking her pulse. Suddenly, she sat straight up in bed and her eyes looking past Daddy were straight and clear. For several weeks, because of her weakness, Mother had not been able to sit up. Also, her eyes had been dreadfully crossed. At that moment, we all knew that she was looking where we could not see and she said clearly, "Yes?" I knew! I think we all knew! She was answering to the call of her name!

"Oh, death, where is your sting?"

His Joy!

His joy is our strength, we shall not be moved.
We can be satisfied with Jesus, His Word is our food.

He refreshes the weary, and satisfies the faint.
He sets us free from the captivity of crime and hate.

Freedom from pride, anger, self, and despair
All kinds of sin and wrong thoughts bring a snare.

But better than life are God's love and His peace.
It's in His presence; we'll find true release.

When we receive daily His bountiful, vast supply
There is food enough for us all that will completely satisfy.

Living Water to drink at the table we see.
The thirsty come seeking, for this water is free.

So, let's lay aside anything that hinders and binds us.
And keeps us from knowing this joy that would find us.

God's grace satisfies and will set us all free.
Jesus paid for our sin when He died on the Tree.

And His joy comes to all who have made Him their Lord.
Let's worship and praise Him, He is Christ our adored!

ALL THINGS NEW
Chapter 8

"I will fear no evil."

"That I may know Him and the power of His resurrection and the fellowship of His sufferings, being conformed to His death..." (Philippians 3:10)

As we settled into our new "home", the Tbilisi State University Hotel, I still was not prepared for the cold that seemed to seep into every cell in my body! The hotel was located in the oldest area of the city; built on the side of a 100-foot cliff where the Kura River ran below. We crawled into bed with our clothes on for a few hours of badly needed sleep. Our Director Merob said that he would be back to take us on a tour of the city in a few hours.

When I awoke around 10 AM, I found Dusty asleep on the hard wooden floor beside our bed without a blanket or pillow! I will never forget the feeling of disbelief that he had to suffer so much. He had a room across the hall, as did Dathan, but I realized how terribly alone they must feel in this strange and cold place that was not like anything they had ever known.

It wasn't until later that we understood that Russia had recently turned off the gas to Georgia. During our first days in Tbilisi, we found that the radiators in every flat and building were still just a tiny bit warm, but the concrete walls were icy cold and the small electric heaters did very little to penetrate the bitter cold. The electricity was seldom on and water was also very unreliable. Our sons and Earl took cold baths, but I could not. The hot mineral baths were close by, but they were dark and gloomy places.

The last time I went there, a rat ran over my bare foot. Suffice it to say, I was disgusted.

Washing the boys' jeans and bedding with a wash board in our bathtub with freezing cold water was not a pleasant experience; nor is it one I recall without some remembrance of the pain my hands endured.

To get to our shared kitchen we had to go down one flight of stairs and outside. Then, we had to go around to the back of the house and down another flight of stairs to the underground kitchen. It was cold and damp. We took turns using it with the landlady who lived downstairs below our rooms.

The first morning in our new home was filled with new sights, sounds, and smells; all so foreign and strange. After a short rest, the first place our Georgian director took us was the ancient and beautiful Sioni Cathedral. It seemed terribly foreign to us. Huge, cold, dark, and impersonal.

It was early afternoon and few people were still worshiping. An elderly woman taught me to make the sign of the Cross. She frowned at me for not already knowing how to do this! In spite of this, I remember feeling very close to God in that church and wanting to pray. We all experienced a reverent awe as we gazed at this magnificent, very old cathedral, and witnessed the richness of the Orthodox worship.

After our time at the cathedral, we were taken to a cave restaurant which we later learned was very Georgian. The air was damp and extremely cold. I wondered how the women who waited on us could stand working in this environment. The food was spicy and foreign, but we ate heartily. We learned later to enjoy the Georgian cuisine, but that first dinner seemed quite spicy and strange. I was surprised to see that I was the only woman eating there. Later, we realized that just the men ate out while it was not accepted for women to go to restaurants to eat. This has changed along with so many other western behaviors that have become accepted by the Georgian people.

The Showing Story

Who would have predicted what was going to happen that cold winter morning in December? We were trying to sell our house, but hadn't had a showing in weeks.

The morning was humming along nicely. Our daughter-in-law needed to run into town for supplies, and since their three children were sick and couldn't go to school, they had come down to our part of the house to hang out for awhile with Grandma and Grandpa.

The oldest, Alex, was on the couch feeling feverish and headachy. Ben was helping me put up more Christmas decorations. We had the tree up and decorated, so most of the storage boxes were back up in the attic. I was soon to know how very fortunate that, at least, turned out to be!

Our two-year old granddaughter, Gracie, was playing quietly with some toys. I was trying to get the medication that I take for Parkinson's disease to kick in so I could make some cookies to take to the neighbors for Christmas. That's when the phone rang.

It was our dear friend and realtor. She said, "You have a showing! They are in La Porte and will be at your place shortly!"

"Please say you didn't say what I think you said!" I replied.

"No, really!" she said. "I only just found out about it myself when the other realtor called to say they would be late."

I began to shake worse than ever; my whole body was trembling violently. "Please, ask them to give us at least 20 minutes," I nearly sobbed into the phone.

I hung up the phone and called out, "We have a showing in just a few minutes! Everybody, pick up your toys and put stuff away! NOW! There isn't going to be enough time to do it all, but let's do our best!"

Alex, from the couch, said, "I can't stand up! I feel dizzy if I do!"

Ben headed up the stairs at a trot, He said, "I'll pick up Gracie's room!"

Earl, moving faster than I've ever seen him move, said, "I've got the kitchen!"

Ten minutes later, the kitchen is looking good,! my roll-top desk is closed to hide my stacks of paper, Earl's desk is clean on top with his papers in a drawer, my little sitting-prayer room has been transformed into a hobby room, and Ben is coming down the stairs calling, "I have Grace's room picked up, but she is taking a bath!"

"Oh, no, you've got to be kidding! Why would she do that?" I asked him.

"I think she heard you say, 'Let's clean everything up!'" he answered with a giggle.

"Well, can you get her out and into her clothes?" My voice was still shaking and too loud which certainly didn't help anything!

That was when we heard the doorbell ring and through the frosted glass of the front door we could see the ladies on the porch waiting to see our house. At precisely the same moment we all looked up to see Ben coming down the stairs. Behind him was Gracie without a stitch of clothes on! It just seemed that she was saying, "Well you did say it was 'a showing,' didn't you, Grandma?"

We all froze for just a couple of seconds, then....YIKES! "Don't answer the door for a minute," I whisper shouted to Earl. "Ben, grab her clothes! Quick! Everyone, let's get up into the attic!"

As we slipped into the upstairs studio room, I heard Earl open the door and let the prospective buyer and realtor in. Shivering, I thanked the Lord for His help as we tiptoed up the steps to the attic.

I nearly panicked again as I realized that I was in desperate need of a drink and there was, of course, no water in the attic. Ben said, "I'll get you some!" It was only a couple of minutes before he was back. "I could only find a sippy cup!" he exclaimed as he handed me the precious water. He also had brought up Gracie's clothes, and they all matched perfectly!

How he did it as a young fellow of seven, I can't say, but one thing I can say is, "Whether you are selling your house or not, there is never a dull moment when you have grandchildren!"

Our 12 Grandchildren

The Great Exchange

It's all in our choices, we make them, each day
These options come before us as we ask, "Which way?"
We need Someone to guide us to Truth in this quest.
"Come unto Me", He said, "And I'll give you sweet rest!"

So, let's trade out the darkness of sin with the light.
Replacing death with life and receiving new sight.
Take hell and judgment; substitute grace and power.
See the thorn, or smell the flower.

If we focus on pain, we'll be ravished by lack.
Let's swap it for the wholeness that He took on His back.
Taking our pain and weakness; choosing to be whole and strong.
Exchanging our weeping for dancing and for singing His song!

Ignorance and confusion transform to wisdom and clear thinking.
If we focus on His Word, we'll rise above and not be lost and sinking.
Fear and doubt, let's trade them out for faith and hope, today.
We'll listen and be careful; very careful what we say!

May we take cold and heartless for warmth and caring instead?
Our hopelessness shall turn into hope, for this is what He said!
And when we're sad and lonely; He'll give us joy and peace.
Not focusing on our lack, our prosperity will surely increase.

There's love for hate, so we'll love others and forgive.
In His presence, all anger is gone and we'll learn how to truly live.
Forgiveness can be easy with His Spirit to guide.
His power to cast away fear when He is by our side.

So, as the worm becomes a pretty butterfly;
We'll become free; if we get rid of the big "I"!
Yes, we'll invite the Lord Jesus there in our place.
"The Great Exchange" is easy when we look upon His face.

The love that He has for us will lift us from despair.
We'll repent of pride and selfishness as we go to Him in prayer.
He will fill our hearts with delight as we become humble and meek.
Exchanging our darkness into light for Christ is who we seek.

Like Moses, or David, or Paul in his cell.
We'll sing the high praises and worship Him well.
He has taken our lives that were once filled with sin.
Cleansed and redeemed us so that new life could begin.

OBEY AND BE BLESSED
Chapter 9

"For you are with me."

"…it is God who works in you both to will and to do for His good pleasure." (Philippians 2:13)

"To them that have no might He increases strength." The dictionary says that strength is "the necessary quality required to deal with stressful or painful situations." May He take us out of our complaining and fill us with psalms of praise; for *"the joy of the Lord is our strength."* His words come back to me as I consider the next step in our ministry for Him: "How do Georgians make good wine?" Often when I feel the squeeze I remember and say, "Just don't let them see the vessel, but only the Wine."

We cast upon Him all of our burdens, our pain, and all of our cares as we consider that unless we keep our hearts right and pure, we will lose fellowship with our Lord and we will be crushed! Jesus is our hope and our crown. Serving Him is a delight when it is the fruit of our abiding in the Vine!

So, living in His faith and not allowing ourselves to live in fear, we obey His call and go forth! We must go as we are compelled by His great love for people everywhere! "Arms of love reaching around the world" mean to us that we must go and tell of the great things that He has done and will do if they believe and receive His incredible love for each one!

"Only twenty-four students! That is all that I can handle!" I had spoken forcefully to the Vice Minister of Education who was our director for the first Christian school that we were starting in Georgia. These students did not know English and I was certain they would need a lot of individual help.

However, Dr. Marob didn't seem to hear. He continued to bring students to my class. Finally, when he brought my 37th student, I convinced him to stop! We began to prepare the two rooms we were renting from a kindergarten in the city for school.

The first day of school was just three weeks after we had arrived in Georgia, March 15, 1992. We had started three schools in Russia; (one in Moscow, one in Alexander, and one in Dubna) before we were able to travel down to Georgia. So many times we saw God do miracles in these schools and we learned so much, as well.

From those experiences, I had a pretty clear idea how to start the first ABC class in what was to become "The School of Tomorrow/Georgia." I taught my students many English songs and games and we made flash cards to teach five new English words and phrases each day. Soon, my smart Georgian students were able to understand simple English phrases and we were on our way to becoming The School of Tomorrow/Georgia, the first English/Christian school in Georgia.

School of Tomorrow/Georgia Students.

The Long's Peak Climb Story

It was a warm summer afternoon, just one year after we had moved to Colorado from our farm in Kansas. We loaded our car with bedrolls, plenty of Gatorade and granola bars, and the guy's sturdy, hiking boots. Six-year old Dusty and I were taking Earl and all four of our other sons up to the trailhead of the over 14,000 ft. majestic Long's Peak where they would meet the folks that had come out to Colorado from our church in Kansas. They were all planning to make the grueling climb to the top the next day.

At the last minute, I had decided to run in and grab my tennis shoes in case Dusty and I decided to do a little hike. My flimsy sandals weren't meant for hiking. I also picked up a light sweater as it often would turn cool up at the higher elevation.

As we drove into the camp-site at the Long's Peak Trailhead, our former pastor from Kansas ran to greet us with a big smile shouting, "Oh, great! You came to join us, Jan!" I quickly assured him that I was just dropping the guys off and wasn't planning to make the climb!

Yet, when he said, "Janie, you can do this!" it seemed to me that it was the Lord speaking through him. Then, when Earl showed me on the map that the "Keyhole" was relatively close to the summit, I said, "Alright! Let's do it, Dusty!"

Earl had also said, "You and Dusty can do it!" This confirmed to me that God was asking Dusty and me to make the climb along with our whole family!

After three or four hours of restless sleep in the back of our van, we joined our Kansas friends for a quick breakfast of donuts, coffee, and orange juice. It was 2:30 AM when we all started the climb. I will never forget the feeling of adventure as I breathed in the invigorating clean mountain air on that moonless still summer night! It was just cool enough that the sweater I had brought with me felt good and my tennis shoes were perfect for the long climb ahead!

As I looked up at the miles of trail snaking up and up above us, I could see other flashlights flickering on the rocky path and hear the low voices of our fellow climbers! To be part of such a courageous and spirited army of people out to conquer this huge and glorious mountain was exhilarating! It was especially grand to know that all seven of our family was on the mountain together!

There is nothing like watching the sun rise from the "Boulder Field"! And then...there it was- the Keyhole! For Dusty and me, this was the top of the mountain. It seemed we could see forever and in the stillness of my heart, I was singing with joy and gratitude for the opportunity and strength to make this climb together with my men! Many folks stopped to admire Dusty's pluck. Although it was a painful climb, without a doubt I knew that the Father had led us to trek up Colorado's most stunning Long's Peak that day in late summer, 1986. I wouldn't have missed the experience for the world!

Two days later as I was jogging, I looked at Long's Peak shinning in all her glory in the distance,. I asked the Lord, "Why did you ask me to climb one of the highest and steepest mountains in North America with my six men?"

He answered in a voice that to me seemed nearly audible, "I want you to know that in your lifetime I will not ask you to climb any mountain unless I have prepared you for it. I will give you the strength, the grace, and all that you need to overcome or surmount anything I call you to do for Me! Do not fear, for I will help you do it!" He said.

When I was a girl on our Kansas farm, I would often play the piano for my father and me as we sang the old hymns. I remember the words to "I Would Be True", and "Send the Light.".

From that time, I determined to live this way and still this is my goal.

Life through Obedience

Obedience to His Word
There is no other way.
To walk in peace and hope in love
Each and every single day.

You must not tarry longer.
Get up, My child, and go.
Take My message to the hungry.
The seeds of Truth you soon must sow.

Delight yourself in My nearness.
Die to self and live in Me.
I'll lead you through the darkness.
Into the Light that sets men free.

Your steps will be quite sure.
Going forth in My light..
On earth no safer place for you
Than where my will for you is right.

Won't you tell about My love.
Speak it wherever you are sent?
For My love is a perpetual fountain.
To all who would receive and repent.

Break loose from the fetters that bind you.
And praise Me in worshipful songs.
Singing in your hearts to Me always.
Victory will be yours all your life long.

Love Whispers

Love whispers come
often in the storms or right after.
Our noisy complaining drowns out the words so that even the melody
Is stolen.
Where?
How can we get them back?
Worship.
A love feast with the Master.
He calls us to come and dine at His Table.
Love whispers are there
At His supra supreme.
Come
He calls us.
Together we dine with Him.
In His love.   jt

("supra" Georgian word for a Georgian feast)

WORRY IS A SIN
Chapter 10

"Your rod and your staff they comfort me.".

"Be anxious for nothing." Philippians 4:6a

We had studied Psalm 91, and the Bible study that I had twice a week for our school staff was officially over. However, one of our precious teachers had stayed a bit later. We were sharing about the faithfulness of God and she was telling me how she needed God's strength and help in the things she was facing in her life. It was wonderful getting to know this lovely teacher who had never opened up to me before.

I glanced at the clock, as I noticed the approaching dusk. Why hadn't Earl returned home?

Where was he? He had left right before the ladies arrived to go on a walk and get his hair cut.

He should have been home, I thought a bit anxiously!

My friend noticed my, concern and said as she left quickly, "Don't worry. I'm sure he is OK!"

As I kissed her check in a Georgian good-bye, I reminded us both of the lesson about safely abiding in the presence of our God.

Yet, my heart was beating rapidly and my hand shaking as I dialed his cell number. No answer! I dialed again and, still, no answer! On the third try a male Georgian voice answered and my voice quavered as I shouted, "Earl?"

After a long moment, he answered, "Hello!"

Relieved, I squeaked out nervously, "Where are you, Hon?"

"I'm not sure." He sounded so confused and weak, but not distressed.

I felt powerless and vulnerable! Fear engulfed my heart and mind as I asked, "Are you hurt? Did someone hurt you?"

"No, I'm not hurt", he replied in that strange child-like tone.

"Who are those men who are with you? What are they doing to you? Did they give you something to drink or eat?"

He just kept telling me he was fine and would come home as soon as he figured out where he was sitting. He confessed that he felt dizzy and couldn't find his glasses but, "No, I'm not hurt!" he tried to assure me.

I felt so completely powerless and I hated to hang up the phone for it was my only link to his whereabouts and though I knew there were men with him, I didn't trust them, nor was my Georgian good enough to converse with them anyway.

"We need to hang up, Honey." I told him. "Hang up your phone and hold onto it! When it rings, answer it! Don't let anyone else answer it! Do you understand?"

He assured me that he did and yet, he sounded so confused!

I hung up and my hands were shaking so much I could hardly punch in the numbers to our friend Gia's cell phone! After several tries, he answered and I fairly shouted, "Earl is in trouble! I don't know where he is! He has his cell phone! Please, see if you can get him to answer!"

Just two years before Earl had been mugged as he went to get a phone card around 9 PM or so in the evening. He had been hit across the face and knocked out! They took his cell phone, wedding ring, wallet with $100 in it along with his Passport, leaving him in a pool of blood on the street!

I was not with him on that trip to Georgia, but his description of that terrible assault made me very aware of the real threat of being robbed and hurt in a city full of desperate and lawless people who would do just about anything to get money for their starving families.

About twenty minutes went by as I read my Bible, walked the floor, and prayed. Suddenly, I felt a peace and I sat down and waited with a sure knowing that Earl was going to be alright. The phone rang and I was relieved to hear Nino, our dear friend and the director of our school, tell me that they had found Earl. He had indeed been hurt! Again, he had been beaten and robbed, this time worse than before, and they had taken him to the hospital.

Soon, she and her husband picked me up and took me to the hospital where he was being treated. He had been hit across the lower cheek and mouth, much as he had been hit in the assault before, and they were stitching up his lip and inside of his mouth. The doctor ordered x-rays to be taken of his head. The hospital had recently purchased a powerful, modern x-ray machine. They found that he indeed had sustained a bad concussion and would need to stay in the hospital for a few days.

The room where they took us was newly remodeled and had a private bath. This was such a surprise to us, as we had never seen a hospital in Georgia so modern and clean! Because it was a newly remodeled bathroom it was very cold and damp, a perfect place to keep our food as it was kept as cold as in a refrigerator. We only had cold water, so showers were out of the question.

We had been made aware of the sad conditions of the medical facilities in Georgia years before when Dusty had to be hospitalized for a week after a freak accident on a sled in Moscow. The hospitals often are not heated and food is not served to the patients, nor is bedding provided. As there isn't adequate nursing care, family members must stay and take care of their ill family members.

After two days and three nights in the hospital, Earl was released to go home, yet he had to stay horizontal for about two and one-half weeks for the concussion to heal. We were so thankful that there were no lasting effects from the mugging! Underneath are His everlasting arms!

It was July 1999, and the words the doctor spoke were still ringing in my ears: "You have Parkinson's disease."

"Are you sure?" I quavered!

"99.9% sure," he answered with authority!

I had not even once considered that this disease might be why my body was doing such strange things. I knew a lot about Parkinson's as my wonderful father had died of it just a couple years before and he had lived with us the last four years of his life. However, when he came to live with us, the disease had advanced considerably more than my symptoms. Neither Earl nor I had even faintly considered that my health issues might be related to this deadly nerve disease.

When I arrived at our home, I walked into our bedroom and laid down on our bed in complete shock! Our youngest son, Dusty came to the open door and asked what was wrong.

"Dr. Schmitt said I have Parkinson's Disease," I answered incredulously! I felt the tears begin to pour from my eyes. I felt many feelings but self-pity and fear were at the top of the list.

"Well, don't worry!" he said confidently, "It's a sin to worry!"

I was amazed at his attitude. The peace and authority of our youngest son's voice brought hope to my fearful heart! I knew that there was nothing that God can not do and no disease could kill me without His knowing! He certainly knew all about what was happening to me. I just needed to trust Him!

Many times, our Lord has healed me or another member of our family! He is always our constant Rock and our Fortress! I had not feared getting this disease or any other! So why did this come upon me? I wondered and fretted, and yet, the words of faith and calmness Dusty had spoken that fateful day in July rang in my ears. "Don't worry! It is a sin to worry!"

CONTENTMENT

Contentment I would give you and yours today.
Receive it with joy, do not fear, I say.
I want you to follow in all that I do.
And My will you must choose to obey.

Don't look back to get My direction.
Nor look to the day before.
For I'll lead and guide each step that you take.
Until I'm exalted and time is no more.

My love is a perpetual fountain.
You don't earn it nor work for My grace.
Oh, the wonder of all that I'll give you.
When you continually seek My face.

Today is a new day for you My child.
Don't hesitate and do not hold back.
Be prayerful and know that I love you.
In Me, you shall find there's no lack.

Break forth the fetters, cast off the chains.
Walk forth in the strength that I give.
Like a fragrant garden after the rains,
Others will follow and learn how to live.

The Lord will guide you continually and satisfy your soul in drought and
strengthen your bones. You shall be like a watered garden, and a stream of
water where waters do not fail. **Is 58:11**

My Song

Singing a new song of praise to our God,
Loving Him more every day.
Nothing can destroy the faith that we have
In our Master and King as we humbly obey.

You, only You, are worthy of praise,
You created all things.
We join with all nature and the angels in heaven
Singing, "Holy is the Lamb who was slain!"

You spoke those words not long ago:
"The Master hath need of thee."
Again I went forth to follow Your call
Helping others to hear and to see.

The darkness flees when the Light comes in
As we all continue to sing.
The delight of those who receive your touch
Keeps us coming and loving as new hope we bring.

Under His Wings

Under His wings, I will always abide.
What He said is true and He stays by my side.
For life in Christ is filled with hope and delight.
He will not fail us, our battles He surely will fight.

Under His wings, there is safety from fear.
It is there we can rest and He'll dry every tear.
I give Him my questions and all of my pain.
His words of love we hear again, and again.

"Come under My wings", He calls each of us.
"You need not tremble with worry or raise such a fuss.
For under My wings I protect and I keep
I shield from all harm, whether you're awake or asleep."

RIGHT THOUGHTS PRODUCE RIGHT BEHAVIOR
Chapter 11

"You prepare a table before me in the presence of my enemies."

Philippians 4:8

Finally, brothers whatever is true, whatever is noble, whatever is right, whatever is pure, whatever is lovely, whatever is admirable if anything is excellent or praiseworthy, think about such things.

The doorbell rang just as our family sat down to dinner in our little green kitchen in Georgia. We were living in a small flat on a busy street in Tbilisi. Reeta, who later became Daniel's precious wife, was with us a lot of the time, as well. Our flat was called a "three-room flat" and with six of us we were a bit crowded, but not as much as so many families in the city. I do not remember anyone complaining about how close we all were to one another.

I heard Daniel ask someone to come in and we all went out to see who had stopped by. It was the 15 year-old girl who lived below us. In her hands was a beautifully decorated birthday cake and we all knew it was for Dathan as today was his 17th birthday.

We all complimented her on the excellent job she had done as she announced that she had made the cake by herself and we invited her to join us for dinner. After dinner, we all had a piece of the delicious cake and enjoyed talking and laughing with our lovely young neighbor. She came up to visit Dathan quite often. He would talk about the Bible and salvation through belief in Jesus Christ. She had many questions and was so open to the Holy Spirit in her life.

A year later, Earl and I were attending one of our American teacher's Bible studies being held on Sunday morning. After the message, we divided up into small groups to pray and our neighbor joined us to make our little circle of prayer. When it was her turn to pray, she said, "Jesus, I am coming home!"

It wasn't long before she was writing poetry and growing in her faith! Her life continues to reflect the beauty of our Lord! She makes careful choices and has become a successful business woman in Georgia. Yet, when we visit with her, she is still the humble sweet girl that we learned to love so many years ago.

Several nights later, friends from Colorado were visiting us when suddenly there was the sound of machine gun fire directly below us on the sidewalk. Our dear friend, Anita, hit the floor and pulled Dathan with her and we all laughed so hard we were crying. From the floor she looked at us in disbelief. We told her that, although this didn't happen every night, it was often and we had to get used to it or we would be so scared we wouldn't be able to stay!

She seemed to take a deep breath as she said, "Well, then, I must just get used to this adventuresome life in wild Tbilisi, Georgia!"

After that, she never showed any fear, even when she was stuck on the horribly crowded metro (subway). It was dangerously crowded and when the electricity went out it was hard to breathe. She and her husband followed the other passengers as they walked down the dark tracks to get out. There were many times when there was no water, no gas, and no electricity, yet this dear friend never complained or grumbled. What a blessing these folks were to all of us as they encouraged us to persevere!

It was several years later, that this same couple traveled back to Georgia with us and several others for a prayer journey. Because she had shown such tenacity and was so flexible, God called Anita and her wonderful husband, Steve, to return to Georgia and with us to combat the wicked forces that have held so many captive in this country for so long!

Just two years after our prayer journey to Georgia, Michael Saachashvili led a revolution that became known as the "Rose Revolution"! The corrupt government was over-thrown without any bloodshed at all! Would this have happened without our prayer journey? I am convinced that it would not! Only God knows what a difference this concentrated prayer for seven days made in individual lives in Georgia, as well as the political moves that have happened since that time. We won't know what evil forces were thrown out of beautiful Georgia because of the powerful move of the Holy Spirit that the seven of us unleashed over the land.

Words

Watching what we say, every single day.
How do our words sound when pain seems to ever abound
And we just can't seem to find our way?
    Kind words.

Today, oh, just for today, I want to say
Words of life, words of joy, lifting and loving every girl or boy
Man or woman that I meet on the way.
    Loving words.

In the power of the tongue is life; there is no horrid spite.
If we learn how to love with the wings of a dove
And speak only what brings our Father delight.
    True words.

Pure words and words that are right teach us how to live in the light.
To live for Christ we speak with humble hearts and meek.
As onward we go ever seeking to know how to fight.
    Faith words.

The power of words bring conviction and trust in a God of sweet diction.
He'll use all of us as we speak what we trust
For the Word is the truth; it is not fiction.
    These are the right words.

"The power of life and death is in the tongue." (Proverbs 8:21a)
"Pleasant words are a honeycomb, sweet to the soul and healing to the bones."
(Proverbs 16:24)

She was lying to our teacher and I couldn't believe it! I was six years old and in the first grade at Waverly School. Waverly was a one room school that Grandpa Morrison had helped to build on the corner just one-fourth mile from our farm. Grandpa had built the first smaller schoolhouse on that same location and although he was only allowed to complete the second grade, he helped build the school that my brother Billy and I attended. It had a wash room where there was a big crock of fresh water the older boys got from the well each morning. We all drank from the one big dipper. On very cold days we did our lessons sitting close to the big old black coal stove that towered over in the back of the large class room.

She was in the second grade and she told the teacher that I was just fooling around and that is why I was late coming in from recess.

It was the first time I remembered hearing a lie and I just couldn't believe it! I told the teacher emphatically, "She locked me in the toilet and I couldn't get out!" I started to cry again! It had scared me so badly when the door would not open. The older girl had pulled the lock down while I was in the toilet and I had finally broken it by hitting it hard with my shoulder. I remember the darkness and the feeling of fear that I would never get out of that awful dark and smelly place.

Then, the worst thing of all happened. My teacher didn't believe me! She didn't believe the other girl either. When my teacher told us she was going to spank us both I was devastated! I do not remember getting but one other spanking in my young life!

The other spanking I received came from my mother because I had disobeyed her. I was three years old and I wanted to call my girl friend who lived next door. My mother told me that I couldn't call her right then. She went outside to hang up the clothes on the line and I remember pushing the chair up to the old crank telephone that hung on our dining room wall. I knew how many cranks to make to call my friend and as I was talking to her, my mother came in and caught me disobeying her! I knew I deserved the spanking and Mother spent time talking to me about why she had to discipline me.

However, the incident at school was so totally different! It took years before I was able to forgive this teacher for her behavior to me that day! I didn't have such trouble forgiving the girl, but a teacher, an adult with authority, that was a different matter.

I wish that I had received teaching long ago about respecting authority that is over us. It would have been so freeing and I would have saved myself some wrong reactions to authority later on that brought me into bondage in my life. Speaking against my teacher brought me sympathy from my parents and grand-parents and fed my self-pity. So, whenever someone hurt me or did something I thought was not very smart, I would talk against them and others would agree with me and this gave me a feeling of power. Well, now I know that this is a false power and instead of freeing me, it brought me into a kind of bondage. Now I see it was the sins of pride and self-righteousness.

Critical words toward those in authority over me were often on my tongue. If those in authority did not behave in just the way I thought they should, I would speak against them, if only in my thoughts. I was not taught that it is the position of authority that I should reverence. Of course, if they ask for something that is against the Word of God, I will "obey God rather than man."

Oh, but the patience and faithfulness of our Lord! Thank God for His mercy and grace! I have finally come to realize that forgiveness and humility are prerequisites to true peace and to the pure worship that my blessed Savior so desires from me. Worship coming from a humble heart bring hope and peace.

More about Words

Words. To me words are fascinating. They can be weapons in our arsenal against the enemy of our souls. Some early mornings I am awakened by the Spirit with a new word. Other times the word comes through the dictionary.

It all started with the word *"tryst"*. To my knowledge, I had never heard this word before. I got up. It was 2 AM. The word means: "A set time and place where two lovers meet." I knew then that God was calling me to meet with him at this time each morning. I fixed up a small "tryst room" in our house and day after day or *"diurnally"* I go there to meet with our Lord.

The following are some of my journal entries using the new words that I especially like:

Today, I am not so *verdant* (a fresh and flourishing condition), but instead am *dulsatory* (lacking in consistency, or order; disconnected). In place of these, I would obtain *equipoise* (balance) and become more filled with *brio* (vigor, life, animation). I will *invigilate* (keep watch) on a *diurnal* (daily) basis.

With *celerity* (quickness in motion or action) help me to be *refulgent* (shining brightly) and *puissant* (powerful, strong and mighty) through the power of the Holy Spirit who lives within me.

One early morning, I was awakened with the word, "*reservoir*". Just writing it makes me feel refreshed. Before I looked it up in the dictionary I meditated on the meaning of this word. I knew it meant more than just a "holding place for water" or as the dictionary says, "a natural or artificial place where water is collected and stored for use, esp. water for supplying a community. I wrote in my journal, "Reservoir- a place where something of value is kept until someone has need of it." I love this definition. We should all be reservoirs for the Lord. Our lives ought to be filled with the things that others may need, like the eight fruits of the Spirit, hope, or wisdom.

When the water in a lake reservoir becomes filled with soil and muck, it must be drained, and then dug out so that the fresh, clean mountain water will have a place to be kept. Likewise, our spirits can become filthy with sin and earthly concerns and cares. We need to *acquiesce* (accept or consent without objection) to the Holy Spirit's *efficacious* (effective, bring about desired result) moving in our lives. It is only then that we will *ameliorate* (make life better for others, improve) other's lives and bring glory to our Lord.

I love the story in Daniel about King Nebuchadnezzar. It is all about a man, a King who was filled with pride and arrogance. He had an image of gold set up for all to worship. The King told everyone in his kingdom that anyone who did not worship the image would be thrown into a fiery furnace. Daniel's friends, Shadrach, Meshack and Abed-negro refused and testified to the king, "O Nebuchadnezzar, we have no need to answer you in this matter. If this is the case, our God whom we serve is able to deliver us from the burning fiery furnace, and He will deliver us from your hand, O king. But if not, let it be known to you, O king, that we do not serve your gods, nor will we worship the gold image which you have set up."

The king was furious and had them thrown into the fire. The fire was so hot that it killed the men that threw them into it, but these men of God did not even smell like smoke. The king watched as they *adulated* (worshiped) God and were not consumed by the fire.

And he said, "Did we not cast three men bound into the midst of the fire?' They answered and said to the king, "True, O king." "Look, he answered. "I see four men loose, walking in the midst of the fire and they are not hurt, and the form of the fourth is like the Son of God."

Just like these three Hebrew men who were *emancipated* (set free) by our Lord Jesus Christ, so He would loose us and show us His salvation.

Oh, that He would help me not to use *logorrhea* (pathological incoherent speech; incessant or compulsive talk), but may I be like Daniel and his three brave friends, *efficacious* (effective; bring about desired results) in every area of my life.

Renew me, Holy Spirit, for in your presence is fullness of joy. At your right hand are pleasures forevermore Because I have set You ever before me and at my right hand is where You dwell, my heart is glad, my spirit rejoices, and my body shall rest secure. I dwell in safety by You for You shelter me all day long. Between Your shoulders is my resting place.

Martha and Mary

"Jesus, Jesus! Don't you see?
She's not helping at all, poor over-worked me!"

"Martha! Martha! Look into My eyes.
My love for you reaches into the skies!"

"Mary! Mary! You chose the best part.
I'll be with you forever and, no, I'll never depart."

"Daughter! Daughter! You worship me well.
I'm dancing over you with joy, can you tell?"

"Children! Children! Come back to Me.
Just sit at My feet and listen, then you will see."

"Beautiful! Beautiful! Your touch is so real.
You lay Your hand on us and place there Your seal!"

Luke 10:38-41

ABOUNDING LOVE
Chapter 12

"You anoint my head with oil"

Philippians 1:9 *"And this I pray, that your love may abound still more and more in knowledge and all discernment.*

We all felt such hope and excitement that lovely spring day in 1993 when Earl and Daniel came into our tiny kitchen and told us about finding "The"perfect place for our Christian school."

"It is in the children's park that is right in the center of the city!" they shared with us over dinner. "There are some dilapidated buildings that appear to be stables for horses and an octagonal building that must have been where horses were shown."

"The park is pretty much run-down and abandoned, but it was dedicated to the children of Tbilisi and it should be built back into a beautiful place where children can learn and grow into great leaders for Georgia." Earl explained. "We so need a building of our own that is just for the school."

It had been a tough job, keeping up with the six locations for The School of Tomorrow/Georgia that year. We had brought three couples and two singles to help train and teach in the six locations. All of the schools were in Kindergarten buildings and it was difficult working with the Kindergarten directors and training the staff in each school. We often talked of how much less complicated it would be if we could have our own building where all of the students could be taught in one location.

Earl and Daniel shared with the family how they had prayed over this very site. Many years ago a seed was planted that would bring forth fruit in the future. We just did not know how much nor how wonderfully God would provide.

Three years later, Earl and I were in Colorado Springs attending a seminar. It had been an inspiring and helpful meeting. As we drove out of the city, Earl mentioned hearing of an organization called EMI (Engineering Ministries International). This organization was formed to help missionaries build schools or churches in other countries.

He pulled the car over to the side of the road and looked through his billfold for the card that someone had given him with the name of an engineer who worked for this unique ministry. Earl found the card and called the EMI number on the card. A friendly, warm voice told us to come on downtown where we might talk. We spent a couple hours sharing with this wonderful man about our ministry to the children of Georgia and he introduced us to the staff and told how they might be able to help us by sending out information to the list of volunteer engineers who were willing to go and help wherever God would send them.

This was the start of the building of the new School of Tomorrow/ Georgia in Msouri Park!

Around a year later, we brought seven engineers and one wife to Georgia where we showed them the area in the park where we had been given permission to build. It was not the area where Earl and Daniel had envisioned the school to be built. It was on a hillside near the entrance to the park. These dedicated and loving people spent several days drawing up plans and putting together the first architectural drawings of the school.

Earl hung up the phone in shock. He told us that the manager of the park had said we could have another area in the park. He said this land might be ideal for the school. Earl knew immediately where he was going to offer for the building of the new School of Tomorrow to be constructed! Yes! The acreage where he and Daniel had walked and prayed over, those years before! The seeds that they had planted in prayer were beginning to bring forth the harvest. The Shepherd was leading us.

In the spring of 1999, three of the engineers returned to Tbilisi to draw up new plans for the area of the park where the school was to be built. They spent hours with Earl putting together the architectural drawings that were used by the construction firm we hired to build the school, the following year.

As the land where we wanted to build is close to the area by the Vera River that runs through Tbilisi, we built the foundation about seven feet deep so that the school is positioned upon rock. This house shall stand for it is built upon the Solid Rock, Christ Jesus, for we know that all other ground is sinking sand.

The following was taken from my journal. June 1992

The School of Tomorrow is full of hope.

This school was built not by worldly manna, but by love.

Love for the children of Georgia and love for the God that sent Jesus to die for them.

So we love in deed and in truth.

All for the glory of God!

After washing all of our clothes in our bathtub with water which we heated up with an electric rod, I wrote the following in my journal:

Friday, and, oh, how I need a rest! They put another boy in my afternoon class. Earl told them to STOP! I taught 37 students today! Oh, Lord, I come to You this spring night. My heart is full of thanksgiving and I worship You! I thank You for our new family here-my brothers and sisters and children that love me, all because they have been changed by Your precious Spirit and they see more clearly now since You sent us here. There is no greater joy than knowing that we are in the center of Your will! Oh, yes, there are green pastures and still waters and how you restored my soul! And, yes, there are flowers everywhere! I get gorgeous bouquets daily-more than we have vases for at school. Their fragrance is delightful! Lord, how I love You this night! Thank You for each precious soul, for the hunger they have for the Word, for Truth, and for Life! I ASK FOR MORE WISDOM, MORE STRENGTH, AND MORE TIME TO SIT AT YOUR FEET.

My Cavorting Story! Another Journal Entry:

Saturday night, March 21, 2009, Earl and I went to nearby church. A lady there prayed for my healing. While praying, she saw me as "a fat sheep cavorting across this green pasture!" (She did not know my love for sheep and lambs or that nearly daily for years I have prayed as the sun comes up in whatever country or place in which I wake up. Malachi 4:2 - *"But to you who fear My name, The Sun of Righteousness shall arise with healing in His wings and you shall go out and grow fat like stall-fed calves."* and the New American says *"skip like stall fed calves!"*) The Amplified version. Says: *"But you who revere and worshipfully fear My name shall the Son of Righteousness arise with healing in His wings and His beams, and you shall go forth and gambol like calves (released) from the stall and leap for joy!"*

I looked up "gambol" means "to skip about as in dancing or synonyms are "spring, caper, frisk, romp" She said I was "going bong! bong! bong! across the green grass!"

What a loving, faithful God we serve!

Mrs. Janet with Her Puppet Charlie.

JOURNEYS WITH JAN
Chapter 13

"My cup runs over."

We have no idea how many trips we have made to Georgia in the past nineteen years. Some were without much mishap, but each time we went to Georgia we knew that there would be more adventures and challenges to face as we continue to follow the Shepherd.

There are three such trips that I will forever remember. I have heard it said that the will of God will not take you where the grace of God will not protect you. We have certainly found this to be true for our God is faithful and He keeps His promises to His children.

The Train Trip:

It was in the fall of 1992, that we experienced three-days and three-nights on a Soviet train. We had decided to take the train instead of flying because we had so much luggage and many boxes of curriculum. Traveling by train was certainly much less expensive. Would we have chosen the train if we had known the condition of most trains in Russia? I seriously doubt it.

The men who picked us up in Moscow to transport our team and luggage to the station had gotten lost. Consequently, we flew into the train station extremely late. Our Russian driver had driven crazily right through the heart of Moscow, swerving and changing lanes, speeding through the busy streets of the huge city of Moscow. Although it was only September, there was plenty of snow on the ground.

As we squealed into the parking lot of the train station, I looked out my side window and what I saw there in the snow I will have in my memory forever. A very old man whose legs had been amputated was lying in the snow. I can still see his dreadful expression as he looked up at me as if to say, "Please help me!" I started to open the door of the vehicle to give him his crutches that were lying nearby. He needed someone to help him get out of the cold snow so desperately and I could only pray that someone would come to his rescue soon as people came dashing toward us yelling that the train was leaving and we had to hurry or we would miss it!

In my mind, I can still picture Reeta, our young friend who was going to teach in one of our schools for a year, running as fast as she could. Her pig tails bouncing and carrying a large net bag of all the drinks we would need through-out our journey to Tbilisi.

Our boxes and luggage were thrown on old luggage carts and we were herded into and through the train station. By the time we all had gotten on the train, along with our entire luggage, two suitcases had been stolen and I was in a state of shock at the deplorable conditions of the train. Earl actually was running along beside the moving train and had to throw himself up on it as the train pulled away from the station.

Our team consisted of eleven people traveling from Moscow to Tbilisi in the oldest, most dilapidated and filthy train you could possibly imagine. The thing I remember most about that trip were the horrific smells which came from the totally filthy bathroom which at least 50 passengers had to use. It had not been cleaned for many years so it was covered with a black sickening grime. Also, I can't forget the holes in the floor of the train, the broken windows, and the "clean", yet still very damp bed clothes someone placed on all our cots.

As I have said, we had eleven in our party, one being a little boy of about two years. His parents were going to teach for a year in one of our attendance centers. One of the suitcases that had been stolen held his diapers and bottles, so by the time we reached Tbilisi he was potty trained and no longer needed a bottle. I guess you could say that this sweet little guy grew up on that long journey.

A funny thing began to happen on that incredible journey. Yes, the conductor tried to break into our compartments at night and he did steal a purse. We were very cold the first part of our trip for we could not shut the broken windows, the other passengers pestered us and tried to get into our compartments, bothering our younger ladies, the filth and conditions were the worst any of us had ever experienced. However, our attitudes were changing and for the better.

We were going through a big trial of our faith. The exciting thing was that we began to love the other travelers. Many of them were Georgians and they enjoyed our songs and tried to make friends with us. But even more important was the fact that we became a unit; caring much for each other as we suffered, worshiped and prayed together throughout the long three days and nights on that unforgettable journey. As our old train pulled into the Tbilisi train station, I was grateful for God's obvious protection over us and even a little sad that the trip was over.

God gives grace and makes the darkness light as we obey Him. "Yes, through it all, I've learned to trust in Jesus. I've learned to trust in God."

The Bus Trip:

Later, Earl and I experienced another amazing adventure as we traveled to our beloved Georgia. Again, we were bringing with us many boxes of curriculum. And again, to save money, we had decided to make the trip to Tbilisi from Trabzon, Turkey by bus. We had flown into Istanbul, Turkey where we loaded our boxes filled with school curriculum on a truck which brought them to Trabzon. We flew from Istanbul to Trabzon where we waited for our materials to arrive. We were several days in this Muslim village located on the Black Sea. I remember hearing the unmistakable dissonant Muslim call to worship every few hours during the day and night and the feelings that the sounds evoked in us. The people were open and friendly to us and we enjoyed our walks along the beach.

Finally, our boxes arrived and we put them on the bus we were taking on to Tbilisi. The trip was to take from four to five hours, so we expected to get into Tbilisi around 11:30 PM that same evening. However, we were not taking into account all the problems we would soon encounter.

The ancient bus had not been kept up. The seats did not recline, some of the windows wouldn't open, and there was only one small heater aimed at the driver. Every seat was filled and all of our traveling companions smoked continuously. It was much too cold to open any windows so we had to endure the thick, noxious tobacco smoke throughout the long, tedious night of travel.

We were held at the boarder into Georgia for several hours while the guards tried to get more money from the passengers. We were all taken into a stark room without furniture and very cold while the guards went through the freight going into Georgia. Most of the passengers had little shops in Tbilisi. They had traveled into Turkey, bringing back items to sell in their businesses. We saw $100 bills being placed in passports where the guards slipped them out and into their pockets. At last, they let us go.

However we didn't go far until the suspension of the bus broke. The driver was going too fast on the rough road we were traveling. The rest of that long dark night we were moving at around ten to fifteen mph as the driver was trying to get to a place where the bus could be fixed.

I only remember stopping for a "bathroom break" twice in the nearly thirty-hour journey on that broken-down old bus. Once, we stopped at a filthy outdoor toilet and the other time the driver stopped in the forest. Ladies went one way and the men the other. I preferred the forest. Around three in the afternoon, we stopped to eat at a road-side café.

It was an exhausting journey, one I would hope to never have to duplicate. Although we experienced a lot of discomfort, we were never afraid or without peace. The other passengers were friendly and sympathetic. We knew God was with us and would give us what we needed to get to Tbilisi and our school. We thanked and praised Him as we arrived at the bus station at around midnight the next day.

The Trip to Amsterdam at Christmas.

In the fall of 1992, there was very little electricity or gas in the country of Georgia. Russia had provided Georgia with utilities, but because of the fall of Communism and rise of Democracy, everything was pretty much shut down. I was continuously cold. Some days, when coming home from my classes, I would just crawl into bed with my coat and hat still on, just trying to get warm.

By the time Christmas was near, I had gotten very ill. Many days I went to school with a fever and laryngitis. It was a blessing that my classes were disciplined and the students listened intently to my teaching even though I could only whisper.

Our oldest son, David, was working in Amsterdam as a missionary. We decided to use the nearly two-month winter break for a vacation and go visit him in Holland. Our family was very excited as we prepared to leave on Christmas day!

We had a Christmas party on Christmas Eve and our whole team came to our apartment bringing deserts and snacks to share. Someone brought beautiful swan cream cakes that we found were not fresh. Consequently, two of our sons and our dear friend, Reeta, became extremely ill during the night. With the electricity and water both off, it was a dreadful experience for us all.

I was so relieved when I got out of bed on Christmas Day to find both water and electricity had come on. I was able to clean the flat before we left for the airport that eventful day.

We were scheduled to fly to Moscow at around 1 PM. We arrived at the Tbilisi airport around mid-morning. A newly married couple was already there. They were going to spend the break in Moscow. Unbelievably, there was only one chair in the huge marble icy-cold waiting area. She was sitting on his lap as they tried to keep each other warm. I remember their blue lips as they shivered and waited for our flight to leave.

It was a very long and cold wait. At around 10 PM, we were told to board the plane. It had snowed so we all sloshed through the cold melting snow and ice on our way out to the Aeroflot plane. Every seat was taken. No one left the plane through-out the long wait to get airborne and on our way. There was no water on board and the bathroom was locked. We waited and we waited. After four very long hours, through my half-asleep state, I heard the plane's engines fire up. By this time, we realized that the reason we couldn't get in the air was that that they didn't have petrol. Telephone service was pretty much non-existent, so we couldn't let the man meeting us in Moscow know when we would arrive.

Shortly after 4 AM, we landed in Moscow. It was nearly 9 before we were finally picked up and taken to where we stayed for a few days while we found a place to purchase our train tickets for Holland.

Soon, we found ourselves traveling by train across Eastern Europe. This train was much nicer than the train we had taken to Tbilisi a few months earlier. We asked that we not have anyone else in our compartment. Although, we had to pay more, we thought it would be safer. However, they paid no attention to our request and a young Russian man was placed in our compartment with us. Later, we believed that he was sent by God to protect us. He never slept during the nights, but stood out in the hall outside our compartment door. Because of him we had absolutely no trouble with people trying to rob us on this trip.

It was around 3 AM one morning on that journey when we were awakened by the train stopping abruptly. Moments later, we had a feeling of being lifted into the air. We became quite concerned when several uniformed armed officers rudely burst into our compartment and harshly asked to see our passports. We were relived to find that they were only putting different size wheels on the train to fit the change in the track's size.

The ambiance in the free world was very different from the eastern European countries. Our moods became lighter each mile that we covered. We were excited to see our son, David, with whom we stayed for over a month. He met us in Germany and took us on to Amsterdam in a rented car.

In Amsterdam, David got us settled in a charming two-story house that he had rented from a famous singer. With four young people and the two of us, the house was crowded, but the lovely two-story Dutch house was such fun for our family. All that wonderful month, God blessed us abundantly in this pleasant cozy house and we have such delightful memories of that time.

While in Holland, we visited wonderful museums and took a road trip out to Corrie ten Boom's home in Haarlem, Holland. We traveled by train to visit the windmills a few miles from Amsterdam, shopped in the nice markets, met many of David's friends, took long walks and prayed for the Dutch people, attended church with David, experienced an incredible display of fireworks on New Year's Eve, and had a splendid time together.

For me, the high point of our vacation was getting to see the ten Boom's.

house and clock shop. The house and shop had been preserved since the war. It was a thrill praying on my knees beside Corrie ten Booms' bed.

Again, we thanked God for His blessings. We left Holland and traveled back to Georgia refreshed as our faithful Shepherd had led us *"into green pastures."*

My Life

Jesus came to give us life, Satan comes to kill.
Choosing life, we live to love;
…Sowing seeds of kindness, still.

We only pass this way one time;
To others we must give, life and light through Jesus Christ
…For it's through Him we live.

Every morning is a gift; a fresh and new beginning;
An opportunity to give His love,
…And not to put off living.

May we light this day with love, and fellowship with others.
For tomorrow will be brighter still, if today we live
…Not for self, but for our brothers.

Earl teaching at our Teacher Training at SOT/Georgia

BUILDERS
Chapter 14

"Surely goodness and mercy shall follow
me all the days of my life."

Many folks have called my husband, *"Earl the Pearl."* However, recently, someone called him by a new name! They called him *"Earl the Builder!"* I've been meditating on this and I believe that he was rightly called! Not only has he been about the business of building walls, schools, and houses, but as a teacher for the past forty years, he has been and still is *"the builder of children."*

The fact is that each of us who teach and work with children is a *"Builder!"* We are the builders of lives that will be the great, wise leaders of the future!

Our Son and Baby Daughter

God is calling for the builders to come forth and build; for some of our children have become like broken walls. There are those who are ravished by the world, having no purpose or foundation! They have neither hope nor peace! He is saying to us who are teachers of children, "Arise and build for as I called Nehemiah to re-build the wall around Jerusalem, so I am calling you to be "My Builders of Children."

∾

It seemed such an impossible task, but Nehemiah courageously answered the call and he set his heart, soul, and mind to the task! He answered the Lord's call, "Let us rise up and build," and the Bible said they "set their hands to this good work." It also says, "...the people had a mind to work." (Nehemiah 4:6)

Look with me at how the people of God were granted success in what seemed an unattainable task:

1. They prayed and listened to the Word of the Lord. They were encouraged! *"The God of heaven Himself will prosper us; therefore we His servants will arise and build..."*(Nehemiah 2:20)

2. They did not let their enemies cause them to become afraid or angry, but they were diligent and united in purpose. *"...for the people had a mind to work."; "...our God will fight for us!" "...with one hand they worked at construction and with the other held a weapon."* (Nehemiah 4:6, 17, 20)

3. The "builders for God" were humble and gave glory to God for what they had accomplished. He gave them the victory and, incredibly, they finished the wall in just fifty-two days..."for they perceived that this work was done by our God."

There are many great and glorious buildings in our world; cathedrals of grandeur and glory that bring honor to man. But there is not a building on earth that can compare to the building of a child into a great man or woman! They come to us as "lumps of coal" and it is our job to work with God that each one will become a diamond.

Sveti Tskhoveli Cathedral.

The cathedrals were built by those who few remember. The builders sometimes made enormous sacrifices! In Mtskheta, Georgia, Sveti Tskhoveli is such a magnificent cathedral! On this incredible edifice is carved an arm of a man with a building tool of some kind in his hand. This carving is at the top of one of the highest peaks in this grand structure. It is said that the main builder did such a glorious work and when it was finished he sacrificed his right arm It was amputated as a symbol of the tremendous sacrifice of this builder. Another legend says that they cut it off so that he couldn't build anything else that would ever match this glorious cathedral.

Students Receive New Bibles From Mrs. Janet

We may never see the end result of what our "lumps of coal" have become! However, we can be confident that God sees and knows every child. He will give us insight into how to mold that child into a stunning diamond who uses his or her gifts and talents to better our world and bring God glory that will last for all eternity!

School of Tomorrow Student (A Future Leader?)

The School of Tomorrow from above.

There is a legend of the builder of another magnificent cathedral. The builder carved a tiny bird up under the roof on a beam where no one would ever see. When he was asked why he was doing this, he replied," Because God sees!"

Don't give up; keep building.
For God sees!

"And I will dwell in the house of the Lord forever."

The School of Tomorrow and Mark IV Harvest

The School of Tomorrow (SOT) was founded February, 1992, after we were invited by the Georgian government to bring American Christian education to Tbilisi. We knew it was a rare opportunity to provide a strong academic and character-building program for the Georgian children. We started the school in March of that same year with thirty-seven students. Presently, there are nearly 300 students enrolled in our school. Almost all of our graduates have attended University. Some have been chosen for elite schools all over the world; such as New Zealand, England, Austria, Spain, and the United States.

Mark IV Harvest is an organization that oversees and helps supervise the ministry of The School of Tomorrow/Georgia. The name, Mark IV Harvest, was given to Earl one night while he was praying about our work in Georgia. The story about planting seeds in Mark 4 of the Bible was the inspiration for the name. Our Mark IV Harvest board of directors currently consists of four successful Christian business men that advise and help manage the educational ministry for the children of Georgia.

The SOT provides grades Kindergarten through 12th grade with a rich biblical curriculum. There is a strong emphasis on the English language. The spiritual growth of our teachers and students is as important as the academic side of the school. The school has excellent standards academically and the lives of everyone involved are touched by the power of the Gospel.

We hope to provide a gymnasium for the students as this is now a government requirement for all schools in Georgia. Additional plans have been made for a larger cafeteria to be built. This would allow us to meet the new government requirements for a hot lunch program and would replace the smaller, insufficient cafeteria that we presently use.

No one knows for sure what the future will bring, politically or economically. However, the chance to place high-standard Christian-based education into the heart of Georgia is both unique and vital. It is a privilege and a challenge to minister to the beautiful children of Georgia through Christian education. We are humbled and deeply grateful to God and to our supporters for the opportunity to make a difference in so many lives.

To participate in this exciting ministry, please contact us at the following:
Mark IV Harvest
www.mark4harvest.org
info@mark4harvest.org
jetreat7@gmail.com
Mobile-(970) 412-5486

And David said to his son, Solomon, "Be strong and of good courage, and do it, do not fear nor be dismayed, for the Lord God - my God - will be with you. He will not leave you nor forsake you, until you have finished all the work for the service of the house of the Lord." (I Chronicles 28:20)